Studies in German Literature, Linguistics, and Culture

Vol. 64

STUDIES IN GERMAN LITERATURE, LINGUISTICS,
AND CULTURE

Editorial Board

Frank Banta, Donald Daviau, Ingeborg Glier, Michael Hamburger,
Gerhart Hoffmeister, Herbert Knust, Egbert Krispyn, Victor Lange,
James Lyon, Michael Metzger, Hans-Gert Roloff, John Spalek,
Eitel Timm, Frank Trommler, Heinz Wetzel

Managing Editors
James Hardin and Gunther Holst
(South Carolina)

The Novels of Martin Walser:
A Critical Introduction

Martin Walser
(Photograph by Hugo Jehle, Stuttgart)

Frank Pilipp

The Novels of Martin Walser:

A Critical Introduction

CAMDEN HOUSE

Copyright © 1991
CAMDEN HOUSE, INC.
Drawer 2025
Columbia, SC 29202

All Rights Reserved
Printed in the United States of America
First Edition

ISBN: 0-938100-98-X

Printed on acid-free paper and with high durability binding

Printed by Thomson-Shore, Inc.
Dexter, MI

Library of Congress Cataloging-in-Publication Data

Pilipp, Frank, 1961-
 The novels of Martin Walser : a critical introduction / frank
Pilipp. -- 1st ed.
   p. cm. -- (Studies in German literature, linguistics, and
culture ; v. 64)
   Includes bibliographical references and index.
   ISBN 0-938100-98-X
   1. Walser, Martin, 1927- --Criticism and interpretation.
I. Title. II. Series.
PT2685.A48Z82 1991
833'.914--dc20   91-3437
                                                            CIP

Acknowledgments

Publication of this book was made possible in part by a grant from Lynchburg College. On a more cerebral plane, I am very much indebted to Ms. Nora Pencola, whose incisiveness and terse eloquence in reaction to the manuscript never ceased to amaze me. To both I wish to express my sincere appreciation.

Contents

	INTRODUCTION	1
1	Walser's Early Works	7
2	Walser's Post-1973 Narrative Phase in Context	19
	Walser's Literary Commitment of the Seventies	19
	The Literary Context:	
	Examples of New Subjectivity	26
	The Narrative Perspective	32
	The Internalized Thematics	36
	The Petty-Bourgeois 'Hero'	39
	Selbstbewußtsein und Ironie:	
	The Irony of Petty-Bourgeois Existence	43
3	Self-Destruction of a Damaged Identity: *Jenseits der Liebe*	47
4	Writing an End to Misery: *Brief an Lord Liszt*	55
5	A Clash of Pretenses: *Ein fliehendes Pferd*	63
6	Sexuality and Death; or, The Dialectics of Domination: *Brandung*	71
	The Dark Side of Sunny California: Excursus on *Meßmers Gedanken*	79
7	Oppression Through Self-Discipline: *Seelenarbeit*	83

8 The Remote-Controlled Life of Gottlieb Zürn:
   Das Schwanenhaus   91

9 On the Prowl; or, The Existential Gloom of
   Gottlieb Zürn: *Jagd*   103

10 Emotional Rebellion — Political Stagnation:
   Dorle und Wolf   109

11 CONCLUSION   117

   Works Consulted   127

The following abbreviations of Walser's works will be used for quotations in the text.

    B — *Brandung*
    BL — *Brief an Lord Liszt*
    DR — *Über Deutschland reden*
    DW — *Dorle und Wolf*
    E — *Das Einhorn*
    EL — *Erfahrungen und Leseerfahrungen*
    EP — *Ehen in Philippsburg*
    F — *Fiction*
    FP — *Ein fliehendes Pferd*
    GF — *Der Grund zur Freude*
    GK — *Die Gallistl'sche Krankheit*
    GR — *Geständnis auf Raten*
    H — *Heimatkunde*
    JL — *Jenseits der Liebe*
    MG — *Meßmers Gedanken*
    S — *Der Sturz*
    SA — *Seelenarbeit*
    SH — *Das Schwanenhaus*
    SI — *Selbstbewußtsein und Ironie*
    WS — *Wer ist ein Schriftsteller*
    WW — *Wie und wovon handelt Literatur*

The translations:

    Br — *Breakers*
    IM — *The Inner Man*
    LL — *Letter to Lord Liszt*
    MP — *Marriage in Philippsburg*
    NL — *No Man's Land*
    RH — *Runaway Horse*
    SV — *The Swan Villa*

INTRODUCTION

READERS FAMILIAR WITH THE work of Martin Walser (born 1927) will readily give him his place in contemporary German literature next to Siegfried Lenz (1926), Günter Grass (1927), Hans Magnus Enzensberger (1929), and Rolf Hochhuth (1931) — authors who also spent their formative years amid the turbulences of World War II. All began to publish in the mid-fifties; all emerged from families of no higher status than middle class; all witnessed the post-war economic ideology with a skepticism that has proved prophetic. Refusing to conform to this ideology which would soon evolve into a self-complacency oriented toward affluence, Walser and his contemporaries insisted on the individual's integrity and his right to unhindered self-actualization. But only Walser has transcended the compelling impulse to come to grips with the German past. In his novels Walser is preoccupied exclusively with the present.[1]

Walser's previous work on Kafka, which had resulted in an insightful and critically acclaimed dissertation, pervaded his earliest prose publication, a collection of short stories entitled *Ein Flugzeug über dem Haus und andere Geschichten* (1955; An Airplane over the House and Other Stories). Critics have always stressed the significance of Walser's occupation with Kafka, whose belated reception and rediscovery after World War II proceeded primarily with Walser's short stories. With his first novel, *Ehen in Philippsburg* (1957; *Marriage in Philippsburg*, 1961), Walser escaped his almost obsessive fascination with Kafka. This work marked a point of reorientation for the author in that it painted a critical picture of the general mentality during the German 'economic miracle' of the Adenauer era. With the journalist's critical eye — from 1949 to 1957 Walser had been employed by the South German Broadcasting System — he observed the social and political development of the Federal Republic in his subsequent novels.

---

[1] Thus far Walser has confined his treatment of the historic past to some of his plays. In *Eiche und Angora* (1962; *The Rabbit Race*, 1963) and *Der schwarze Schwan* (1964; The Black Swan) he illuminates Germany's National Socialist past, the history play *Sauspiel* (1975; Sow Game) deals with the German peasant uprisings, and *In Goethes Hand* (1982; In Goethe's Hand) recapitulates cultural history from a contemporary perspective. This book discusses Walser's prose only and excludes his dramatic writings.

Considering his literary activity a historiography of daily life,[2] Walser presents in each of his novels an individual whose life achieves exemplary significance. His protagonists, usually average middle-class men who seem to age in parallel with their author, descend from a proletarian background. In their desperate search for individual happiness they continually succumb to society's dictates, and their frustrations about this dilemma permeates the private sphere of their lives. By tracing the societal origins of psychological deformations Walser discloses the conditions which for his characters invalidate the right to self-actualization. Despite the author's ironic stance toward his characters, Walser admits to his personal relation to their conflicts. Each of his novels articulates the vast abyss between the claims of the individual and the demands of society, between internal and external reality.

This study will provide a comprehensive treatment of Walser's narrative phase from 1976 to 1988 against the background of his entire prose oeuvre. The texts to be discussed are the novels *Jenseits der Liebe* (1976; "Beyond all Love," 1982), *Seelenarbeit* (1979; *The Inner Man*, 1984), *Das Schwanenhaus* (1980; *The Swan Villa*, 1982) *Brief an Lord Liszt* (1982; *Letter to Lord Liszt*, 1985), *Brandung* (1985; *Breakers*, 1987), *Jagd* (1988; *On the Prowl*), the novellas *Ein fliehendes Pferd* (1978; *Runaway Horse*, 1980) and *Dorle und Wolf* (1987; *No Man's Land*, 1988) as well as the collection of aphorisms, *Meßmers Gedanken* (1985; *Messmer's Thoughts*). Apart from their limited reception, the selection of these texts is based on Walser's modified narrative approach after completion of the Kristlein trilogy in 1973.

In his post-1973 prose oeuvre Walser no longer employs the first-person narrator of his earlier novels *Halbzeit* (1960; Halftime), *Das Einhorn* (1966; *The Unicorn*, 1971), *Die Gallistl'sche Krankheit* (1972; Gallistl's Disease), and *Der Sturz* (1973; The Fall), but presents his narratives in the third person while maintaining the figural perspective of the protagonist. Thus, a more internalized and reflecting mode of portraying socio-political issues replaces the extroverted and commenting style of Walser's earlier texts. The disappearance of the first-person narrator brings with it a thematic shift of accent in Walser's prose as it entails the protagonist's progressive loss of self-assertion and disintegrating sense of identity. Whereas a first-person narrator appears to be in control of the narration, the protagonist referred to in the third person is not a narrat*ing*, but rather

---

[2]See Martin Walser, "Wer ist ein Schriftsteller," *Wer ist ein Schriftsteller* (Frankfurt/M.: Suhrkamp, 1979) 25; furthermore Monika Totten, "Ein Gespräch mit Martin Walser in Neuengland," *Martin Walser*, ed. Klaus Siblewski (Frankfurt/M.: Suhrkamp, 1981) 34.

a narrat*ed* subject, and therefore — strictly speaking — dependent on a superior narrating authority.

Underscored by these formal characteristics, the theme of the protagonist's social conditioning and domination by society is no less prevalent in Walser's later works. Walser sketches the theoretical basis of his views on narrative in his most pertinent essay collection *Wer ist ein Schriftsteller* (1979; What Makes an Author), defining his literary commitment of the seventies, which contrasts with the contemporaneous tendency of the so-called 'New Subjectivity.' His persuasions concerning all writing of literature are quite straightforward and adamant. He believes unconditionally that virtually any sort of literary narrative constitutes a reaction to that one painful experience he calls dependency or unfreedom.[3]

Walser's works have not always elicited unanimous applause from the critics. Nonetheless, the massive number of critical responses since the late fifties — both in feuilleton and scholarly reviews — and a growing number of monographs since the early seventies attest to Walser's influence on as well as his importance for contemporary German literature. The most recent (and first bilingual) collection of essays, *Martin Walser: International Perspectives* (1987), is also the first volume on the author published in this country. Following the same critical slant of earlier publications, the majority of essays in this edition inquires into the implicit social political momentum of Walser's works and focuses specifically on the forms of alienation and oppression.[4] This study continues previous scholarly research on the socio-critical tendency of Walser's texts; it examines the nature and effects of social conditioning as experienced by Walser's characters; it furthermore discusses the protagonists' dependencies on their defensive strategies for survival resulting from their dominated and alienated identities. Because external reality is brought to light only through the characters' perception, this topic requires a critical analysis of the psychological interplay between the protagonist and the outside world.

---

[3] See Walser, "Die Literatur der gewöhnlichen Verletzungen," *Die Würde am Werktag: Literatur der Arbeiter und Angestellten*, ed. Martin Walser (Frankfurt/M.: Suhrkamp, 1980) 7.

[4] How radically the views between daily reviewers and Walser's academic reception can differ is documented by an American review of *Breakers*, according to which Walser is "not obsessed by the moral burdens of history; his novels are not ... weighed down by symbolism or political baggage"; Raymond Sokolov, "German Fiction Without Fear," rev. of *Breakers*, *The Wall Street Journal* 17 Nov. 1987: 36. In this particular case, the inference from one novel to the author's entire oeuvre leads to an inaccurate account.

In revealing society's mechanisms within Walser's fictions, Herbert Marcuse's critical theory of society, *Eros and Civilization* (1955) and *One-Dimensional Man* (1964), serves as a critical supplement. Marcuse's approach, too, is a psycho-political one and concentrates on the connection between psychological formations and socio-political structures. It is precisely this correlation, the "nexus between private agony and public nightmare," that Walser has endeavored to elucidate in his novels and novellas since 1976.[5]

According to Marcuse, in an advanced industrial society the reality principle, whose chief social manifestation is work in general and its rigorous principles of production that fundamentally oppose the individual's quest for personal autonomy, has virtually eradicated its antipole, the pleasure principle. The principle of work reality then is antonymous to freedom in that its objectives differ from those of the individual, whose creative potential is forced into non-creative channels. Marcuse's global statement about the working population applies to the protagonists in Walser's novels, who "do not live their own lives but perform pre-established functions. While they work, they do not fulfill their own needs and faculties but work in alienation."[6] It should be noted that Marcuse's utopian perspective of overcoming the repressive performance principle cannot be claimed for Walser's novels, which do not project such an optimistic promise.

Parallel to his prose, Walser has been astoundingly productive as a writer of essays. These texts are relevant in so far as they delineate Walser's evolution as a critic of society in general. While one cannot equate social political reality as portrayed in Walser's essays with the fictional reality depicted in his novels, in Walser's view reality and fiction are dialectical correlates from which he derives his concept of writing. Parallels to Walser's essays shall be noted, especially when — as in the case of his lectures on *Selbstbewußtsein und Ironie* (1980; Self-Identity and Irony) — they reveal additional dimensions of the novels' thematic structures. Thematically, the common denominator of Walser's texts lies in the social origin of the protagonists. It is the petty-bourgeois consciousness of the main character through which Walser mediates external reality. Consequently, his expositions on self-identity and irony, which contain analyses of the protagonists' lower middle-class mentalities in Kafka and Robert Walser, carry programmatic significance for Walser's later novels.

---

[5]Ernst Pawel, "The Empty Success of Herr Zürn," rev. of *The Swan Villa*, *The New York Times Book Review* 10 Oct. 1982: 11.

[6]*Eros and Civilization: A Philosophical Inquiry into Freud* (Boston: Beacon Press, 1964) 41.

It is striking that Walser places each of his protagonists in a different professional environment. This allows him to detect oppressive mechanisms in various locations of the social spectrum. Franz Horn in *Jenseits der Liebe* and *Brief an Lord Liszt* holds an executive position as a business representative, Helmut Halm in *Ein fliehendes Pferd* and *Brandung* enjoys the social prestige of a *Gymnasium* teacher. Similarly, Wolf Zieger in *Dorle und Wolf*, who is employed by the state administration of Baden-Württemberg, is a tenured public servant. Gottlieb Zürn in *Das Schwanenhaus* and *Jagd* makes his living as an independent real estate agent, a profession that is directly associated with the competitive struggle of the free market. It is only his cousin Xaver Zürn, the private chauffeur in *Seelenarbeit*, who finds himself in a an explicitly subordinate social position. Walser rarely presents his protagonists' conflicts as resulting from immediate dependencies, but rather points to the complicated strategies that they have developed in order to cope psychologically with social hierarchies.

In order to critically evaluate Walser's texts several issues appear to be pertinent: the manipulative influence exerted on the individual's psyche by the demands and dictates of a capitalist system; the effects on behavior patterns in both public and private life; and, finally, the question concerning alternatives with regard to the realization of one's individual personality, the development of an individuality untainted by a socio-economic system that seeks to guarantee public wealth by insuring the smooth functioning of the free market instead of directly attending to the individual's well-being and needs. These issues illustrate the problematic and the outlook of Walser's texts and cast light on the author's concept of writing, the function he assigns to literature, and finally the critical potential of his fiction.

1

Walser's Early Works (1957-1973)

ACCORDING TO A STATEMENT in Walser's essay "Imitation oder Realismus" (1964; Imitation or Realism), the insoluble existential predicament in which an individual immersed in a society must find himself consists of the two mutually exclusive alternatives of survival or the discovery of a genuine self-identity. What Walser expresses here is the fundamental antagonism between the notion of self-realization or personal autonomy on the one hand and a social form of existence on the other. Walser rejects the notion that a social individual possesses genuine freedom of choice as society permeates all aspects of his life. No one can withstand the "Konditionierungsmaschinerie Gesellschaft" [machinery of social conditioning] nor avoid being brainwashed by it (EL 67).

Walser's first three novels establish the literary theme which would dominate the socio-political commentary embedded in the characterization of his protagonists. Their commonality rests in their being men whose only and unconditional purpose it is to climb the social ladder, a quest which they consider the path to self-actualization. In these novels Walser sketches a broad social panorama of the fifties and sixties with their materialistic mentality, society's stifling performance pressure, the need for conformity and role playing, as well as the necessity for individual survival strategies. The protagonist in Walser's fiction commonly accepts "societal authority" and assimilates it with his "own desire, morality, and fulfillment," lacking awareness of his progressive alienation.[1] In this fashion his individual desires and inclinations are easily manipulated, "organized," and subjected to the laws of a society based on profit maximization and competition.[2] By curtailing the individual's genuine potential for self-actualization the system perpetuates its own growth. In exchange for the system's "oppressive productivi-

---

[1]Herbert Marcuse, *Eros and Civilization*, p. 42.

[2]Marcuse, *Eros and Civilization*, p. 14.

ty" the individual is offered material compensation and various other services.[3] Thus an enhanced standard of living is the sole restitution for the increasing influence exerted by society. Owing to the intellectual and materialistic capabilities of the system, the offered prospects of self-realization have assumed the function of a "powerful instrument of domination."[4] Therefore the ideology of an advanced industrial society appears to advocate a form of "comfortable, smooth, reasonable, democratic unfreedom."[5] This constitutes the irrational element within an otherwise rational system.

In *Ehen in Philippsburg* the protagonist finds himself entangled in a web of conditioning forces exerted by the regenerated economy of post-war Germany. The economic laws of that system lend themselves to a dualistic view of social reality, polarizing the haves and the have-nots, the mighty and the weak, the free and the unfree. The novel consists of four episodes which are narrated in the third person from the perspective of the respective protagonist. The main character and protagonist of the first and last episode, Hans Beumann, bestows on the novel its temporal and thematic continuity.

After graduation from university Beumann promises himself an effortless social advancement and the fulfillment of his dreams of imminent prosperity — "der geplante Wohlstand" (EP 87). He feels short-changed, however, when he realizes to what extent he is forced to comply with the demands of the system. Yet Beumann persists, his quick opportunism and willingness for conformity being a direct consequence of his proletarian background.[6] An illegitimate child of a waitress, Beumann has never cast off his innate inferiority complex vis-à-vis the financially powerful. With naive admiration he undergoes his first contacts with the Philippsburg bourgeoisie, a society into which his integration would designate self-fulfillment. Although Beumann is superficially aware of social injustice and flaws in the system — "Natürlich war er gegen die Fabrikanten, gegen die reichen Leute..." (EP 57) ["Naturally he was *against* industrialists, against the rich people..."; MP 53] — he lacks any deeper insights into economic

---

[3]Marcuse, *One-Dimensional Man: Studies in the Ideology of Advanced Industrial Society* (Boston: Beacon Press, 1964) 17.

[4]Marcuse, *One-Dimensional Man*, p. 7.

[5]Marcuse, *One-Dimensional Man*, p. 1.

[6]See Klaus Pezold, *Martin Walser: Seine schriftstellerische Entwicklung* (Berlin: Rütten & Loening, 1971) 79.

structures.[7] As he is invariably dependent on the system's benevolence and financial support, Beumann possesses virtually no freedom of choice. Any refusal to conform with the given conditions would forever deny him access to the Philippsburg society.

Upon accepting employment as a journalist Beumann submits his personality to be tailored according to Philippsburg standards. Still exuding a childlike idealism, he cannot resist the system's manipulative influence.

> Die Unternehmer bestimmen mit ihren geschäftlichen Manipulationen die Geschicke der weniger einflußreichen Bevölkerungsgruppen. Ihre Entscheidungen kommen damit einer politischen Bevormundung der unteren Schichten gleich, so daß diese bald ihre eigenen Interessen nicht mehr von denen der wenigen Industriekapitäne zu unterscheiden vermögen. Unterstützt wird dieser Verlauf durch Funk und Presse, die es verstehen, die Nutzen der Wirtschaftsführer auch als Nutzen der Allgemeinheit darzustellen.[8]

[Through their economic manipulations the employers control the fate of the less influential strata of the population. In this manner their decisions equal a political tutelage of the lower social strata, who in turn can no longer distinguish their own interests from those of the few industrial tycoons. This process is promoted by the mass media by effectively passing off the advantages of industrial leaders as being beneficial to the general public.]

Never does Walser's novel create the image of a harmoniously progressing affluent society; it rather demonstrates the power of the capitalists over their subordinates and thus reduces the meaning of freedom to the freedom of capitalist exploitation: "Alle gegen alle, ... das ist Freiheit" (EP 87) ["Everyone against everyone else, ... that is freedom"; MP 80]. Although Beumann in the end manages to be accepted by the Philippsburg bourgeoisie, he nevertheless displays hidden signs of defeat. In order to win his social victory, Beumann had to commit "den Verrat, der den Jüngling zum Mann macht" (EP 61) ["this betrayal which makes the adolescent a man"; MP 57], a crime for which he has paid with the adjustment of his personality. Hence the novel may be considered a counter-

---

[7]Pezold, *Martin Walser*, p. 87.

[8]Heike Doane, *Gesellschaftspolitische Aspekte in Martin Walsers Kristlein-Trilogie* (Bonn: Bouvier, 1978) 19.

example to the traditional German *Bildungsroman*, in that it illustrates not the formation and consolidation of a self-identity, but rather its deformation.[9]

While *Ehen in Philippsburg* centers thematically upon the protagonist's adaptation to the extant social conditions, Walser's second novel *Halbzeit* depicts a more developed stage of conformity on the part of its narrator-protagonist, Anselm Kristlein. Told in the first person, the novel, nearly nine hundred pages in volume, consists of the long-winded, often interminable ramblings of its protagonist, a linguistic exuberance that somewhat counteracts the novel's critical potential.[10] As a young sales agent, Kristlein is trapped between the ruling upper middle class and the dominated lower class, between the grand bourgeoisie and the proletariat.[11] His identity consists of various roles, which he has been trained to produce on demand. Unconscious of the system's grinding machinery, Kristlein blindly heeds the demands imposed on him. Being rigidly controlled by these demands, Kristlein is perched precariously on the verge of relinquishing his own identity, trying to stave off its dissolution into mere "Mimikry," as the novel's first chapter is titled. Although he has not yet succumbed completely to faceless conformity, his behavior patterns reflect a chameleon-like existence in order to assert himself in a pluralistic society.[12]

Once again the system operates much like in the preceding novel. The industrialists (here, the Franzke corporation) take ruthless advantage of their employees, allowing the material compensations provided by the company to veil the feudalistic nature of these working conditions. The employees view the successes of the industrial leaders as a gauge of their own failures;[13] hence they resign themselves to their dependency. Kristlein's existence assumes exemplary significance as he finds himself confronted with and exposed to the competitive struggle for material status and — like Beumann before him — has to accept his powerlessness against the establishment. Yet for him too the feeling of being

---

[9]Anthony Waine, "Martin Walser," *The Modern German Novel*, ed. Keith Bullivant (Leamington Spa: Berg, 1987) 262.

[10]See Manfred Durzak, *Der deutsche Roman der Gegenwart: Entwicklungstendenzen und Voraussetzungen* (Stuttgart: Kohlhammer, 1979) 240.

[11]Ingrid Kreuzer, "Martin Walser," *Deutsche Literatur der Gegenwart in Einzeldarstellungen*, ed. Dieter Weber (Stuttgart: Kröner, 1976) 523.

[12]Hinton Thomas, and Wilfried van der Will, *Der deutsche Roman und die Wohlstandsgesellschaft* (Stuttgart: Kohlhammer, 1969) 114.

[13]Doane, *Martin Walsers Kristlein-Trilogie*, p. 24.

oppressed disappears "in the grand objective order of things which rewards more or less adequately the complying individuals and, in doing so, reproduces more or less adequately society as a whole."[14] Blinded by his one-tracked, profit-oriented mentality, Kristlein inadvertently submits to the disintegration of his personality. Conformism ultimately constitutes the premise of survival.

In *Das Einhorn* the theme of individual alienation is amplified through the more concrete portrayal of economico-political dependencies.[15] Kristlein's frequent referral to the competitive conditions that rule supreme lends tangible credence to the oppressiveness of the circumstances. Because Kristlein still clings to his own social aspirations, however, he cannot detach himself from the competitive principle. In view of a "rising standard of living, non-conformity with the system itself appears to be socially useless, and the more so when it entails tangible economic and political disadvantages...."[16]

Notwithstanding Kristlein's social rise from sales representative to an intellectual of sorts — he now writes for a living — his financial dependency on his contractors continues to exist. Since all his attempts at self-actualization have come to naught, Kristlein is angered with his "dressierte Natur" [conditioned character] (E 307). He recognizes himself as a variety of socially determined components that stigmatize him as a "Divíduum" [dividual] (E 150). Contrary to the earlier novels where the individual's experience of his impotence was ultimately allayed with resignation,[17] Walser for the first time presents his protagonist with an awakening political consciousness, namely when Kristlein envisages his solidarity with his fellow sufferers as a first step toward political action. Yet, even the quest for an oppositional stance turns into another Darwinist struggle for self-assertion. *Das Einhorn* ends with Kristlein's conjuration of a utopian existence after which he remorsefully pledges eternal loyalty and allegiance to his wife.

Whereas the first two volumes of Walser's trilogy illustrate Kristlein's social ascent, the last sequel, *Der Sturz* mercilessly pursues the protagonist's downfall. Kristlein's unstable self-esteem has meanwhile turned into despair about a life the

---

[14]Marcuse, *Eros and Civilization*, p. 42.

[15]Cf. Thomas Beckermann, "Epilog auf eine Romanform. Martin Walsers Roman *Halbzeit*: Mit einer kurzen Weiterführung, die Romane *Das Einhorn* und *Der Sturz* betreffend," *Martin Walser*, ed. Klaus Siblewski (Frankfurt/M.: Suhrkamp, 1981) 103.

[16]Marcuse, *One-Dimensional Man*, p. 2.

[17]See Doane, *Martin Walsers Kristlein-Trilogie*, p. 7.

meaning of which exhausts itself in "Geldverdienen" [making money] (S 26). The fifty-year-old Kristlein, exhausted and disillusioned after many years of excruciating competition, has realized that the necessity for conformity and his quest for personal autonomy have become an insoluble conflict.[18] All the energies to rekindle his desire for political opposition have vanished, and Kristlein finds himself at the mercy of the industrialists. In order to support his family, he has once more accepted employment in a subordinate position, which again points to the causes of his psychological deformations.[19] The realization that his desire to accumulate wealth in order to liberate himself from the social power mechanisms has only made him "immer abhängiger" [increasingly dependent] (S 325) induces him to terminate his quest for independence. Kristlein eventually penetrates the nature of his dependencies and realizes that competition simply promotes the consolidation of the extant conditions.

Already in his earliest essays Walser bemoans the fact that the system works to the advantage of those who possess the power and the capital, while the majority of the population still exists in subordination (H 62). As the number of these "subordinates" is increasing steadily, Walser considers it a most ominous achievement of the free market system to have put a radical halt to the democratization of the blue-collar labor sector. The underprivileged classes are still denied the right for self-determination, and the system has therefore produced a (grand) bourgeoisie that worships itself as the ultimate accomplishment of German, if not human, history (H 63). With this line of arguments Walser tries to draw attention to the enormous discrepancy between (democratic) ideals and social reality.

As to Kristlein's ideals, they are ultimately shattered with his dismissal, synonymous with his social uselessness, and the subsequent vision of his own suicide. Although he recognizes the system's destructive potential, he cannot escape from it, which leaves him in a hopeless dilemma that reaffirms the irreversibility of the social conditions.[20] The never-ending process of Kristlein's social conditioning eventually results in the irreparable deformation of his personality, a theme much cherished by Walser for its ability to facilitate the demonstration of the destructiveness inherent in social policies. Owing to his inability to subscribe blindly to the capitalist ideology and to overtly declare his allegiance

---

[18]See Doane, *Martin Walsers Kristlein-Trilogie*, p. 150.

[19]Anthony Waine, *Martin Walser*, p. 93.

[20]Doane, *Martin Walsers Kristlein-Trilogie*, p. 203.

to the proletariat, Kristlein remains trapped between social classes.[21] Nevertheless, Walser's indictment is directed not only against the capitalist system. Kristlein's mentality as presented in the trilogy is representative of the lack of political perspective in the West German middle class of the sixties and early seventies.[22] To some extent, at least, Walser attributes the blame to those individuals who blindly subscribe to the prevailing ideologies and thus perpetuate the socio-economical conditions. It is thus clear that Walser's perception of the workings of social change presupposes a consciousness in the citizens of its necessity.[23] Only if the given circumstances are perceived as a "state of negativity which is to be negated,"[24] can the humans liberate themselves from the state of oppression.

It is precisely this emancipatory consciousness that Walser illustrates in his novel *Die Gallistl'sche Krankheit* published before *Der Sturz* in 1972. While the Kristlein novels reflect middle-class paralysis, Gallistl points out the solution for this state of political stagnation. Gallistl, a middle-aged intellectual, gives vent to his discontent about the political conditions and his own conformist disposition by writing his own "Krankheitsgeschichte" [chronicle of his disease] (GK 10). A purely cognitive process, the plot is internalized and describes what Kristlein repressed or accepted: loneliness, performance pressure, the need for conformity, in short, socially engendered deformations of the individual.[25] Gallistl can no longer approve of the "Abhängigkeitsgefälle" [hierarchy of dependencies] (GK 29) that exists even among his friends. He has recognized that by submitting to the "Abrichtung" [conditioning] (GK 105) through society and the extant competitive conditions, one only promotes the capitalist mode of production: "Sie ernähren das Prinzip, an dem sie scheitern" [They nourish the principles that will make them fail] (GK 43).

---

[21]Hermann Kinder, "Anselm Kristlein: Eins bis Drei — Gemeinsamkeit und Unterschied," *Text + Kritik* 41/42 (1974): 43.

[22]Heike Doane, "Zur Intensivierung der politischen Thematik in Martin Walsers Kristlein-Trilogie," *Weimarer Beiträge* 30 (1984): 1844.

[23]This coincides with Walser's statements in an interview with Dieter Zimmer, "Die Anstrengung, die das pure Existieren ist," *Die Zeit* 18 May 1973: 27.

[24]Marcuse, *One-Dimensional Man*, p. 66.

[25]Cf. Kurt Batt, "Fortschreibung der Krise: Martin Walser," *Martin Walser*, ed. Klaus Siblewski (Frankfurt/M.: Suhrkamp, 1981) 137.

Gallistl is aware that individual "independence of thought, autonomy, and the right to political opposition are being deprived of their basic critical function" as society appears "increasingly capable of satisfying the needs of the individuals through the way in which it is organized."[26] The resolution to discontinue his quest for material status clears the path for his eventual affiliation with a Marxist group. This "Trennung von sich selbst" [divorce from himself] (GK 86) enables Gallistl to lead a new life style free of the constraints and dependencies of capitalist consumer society. Contrary to Kristlein, Gallistl is now immune to the alienating effects of the "kapitalistische Leistungsgesellschaft" [capitalist performance society] (GK 104). Fortified by his self-liberating actions, Gallistl demands the "entwickelten Menschen" [advanced human] (GK 108), who will elevate himself intellectually above society's manipulative mechanisms that appeal to man's most primitive instincts. A code of societal interactions based on alienation (GK 111) must necessarily breed synthetic identities, a chain which draws parasitic strength from its own success and can only be negated by a socialist consciousness.[27] The fact that Walser himself had for a short time (1972-74) expressed his sympathies with the German Communist Party (DKP) — without actually becoming a member — may account for Gallistl's straightforward creed. The sudden turn of his disease into recovery is depicted in the last chapter. Its fairy-tale title "Es wird einmal" [once there will be] (GK 83) betrays Gallistl's wishful thinking and projects a utopia of Democratic Socialism which in the subsequent novel *Der Sturz* was to revert again to bleakest hopelessness.

Between *Das Einhorn* and *Der Sturz* Walser published *Fiction* (1970), a short, unconventional narrative that has been largely ignored, or — perhaps justifiably so — discredited by readers and critics alike. Unlike in Walser's preceding novels, the narrator of *Fiction* remains faceless and without name. The narration is limited to an often incohesive train of impressions, a plethora of evanescent images — "Eine Menge Bilder" (F 7) — that lack totality and shape the narrator's perception of external reality. Thus the narration follows the reactions of the narrator's consciousness on his way through a city, while the plot remains rather diffuse. Internal and external reality fuse into a pseudo-reality of language, which is then presented as 'fiction,' constructed by a language that questions

---

[26]Marcuse, *One-Dimensional Man*, p. 1.

[27]The criticism has been advanced that Gallistl's political consciousness can only be aroused by a "sozialistische 'deus ex machina'"; see Peter Laemmle, "'Lust am Untergang' oder radikale Gegenutopie? *Der Sturz* und seine Aufnahme in der Kritik," *Martin Walser*, ed. Klaus Siblewski (Frankfurt/M.: Suhrkamp, 1981) 204.

itself. The text abounds with sentence fragments and multiple parodies of idioms and phrases. At the end the narrator withdraws from his fiction and retreats to a mental asylum. The leading impression of the story is that of the narrator's disgust with external reality and his disillusionment with a deficient and static language mirroring the stagnant social conditions.

The ideology of society in Walser's novels discussed thus far is marked by what Marcuse describes as the subversion of individuality through the concomitant rise of materialism:

> [t]he better living is offset by the all-pervasive control over living.... The ideology of today lies in that production and consumption reproduce and justify domination. But their ideological character does not change the fact that their benefits are real. The repressiveness of the whole lies to a high degree in its efficacy: it enhances the scope of material culture, facilitates the procurement of the necessities of life, makes comfort and luxury cheaper, draws even larger areas into the orbit of industry — while at the same time sustaining toil and destruction. The individual pays by sacrificing his time, his consciousness, his dreams; civilization pays by sacrificing its own promises of liberty, justice, and peace for all.... What remains is the negativity of reason, which impels wealth and power and generates a climate in which the instinctual roots of the performance principle are drying up.[28]

With the exception of *Die Gallistl'sche Krankheit* Walser posits no explicit ideology in his novels. Yet his fictions strive for a capitalist realism which is to expose the system's destructive mechanisms. It is both Marcuse's and Walser's concern to protest against the domination of the lower social classes by the ruling class. Both writers hope to kindle new desires in the reader that might motivate or at least make him susceptible to the need of social progress. The failures of Walser's characters, however, provide no reason for optimism, as Walser himself states:

> Im Grunde genommen wäre alles für Demokratie vorbereitet. Der Kapitalismus ist total durchleuchtet, es fehlt an nichts mehr, wir können morgen anfangen, aber niemand ist bereit dazu. Seit 1970 findet geradezu eine Sturzwelle nach rechts und rückwärts statt, obwohl noch nie soviel theoretische Schlüssigkeit in der Überwindung des Kapitalismus hin zur Demokratie bestanden hat. Und warum? Weil das alles nur Meinungen

---

[28]Marcuse, *Eros and Civilization*, pp. 91-93.

und Analysen sind, die keinen Menschen außerhalb der universitären Seminare berühren.²⁹

[Basically everything would be ready for democracy. Capitalism has been completely unmasked, everything is prepared and we could start tomorrow, except no one is willing. Since 1970 we have seen a tidal wave to the right and backward, although we have never had more theoretical proof that capitalism must be abolished in favor of democracy. And why, may I ask? Because all that is only opinions and analyses which do not affect anyone outside of university seminars.]

These words, uttered in 1974, clearly betray the author's disillusionment at that time. Subsequently Walser moved away from the global, panoramic view of society which he had endeavored to capture in his early novels. In the prose works after 1973 he begins to investigate the inner world of his protagonists and to present a detailed, albeit not unproblematic, account of their psychological make-up. Instead of an outside view of society, Walser's narrators assume the perspective of the respective protagonist and write 'from the inside out.' The retreat to the inner world of the character may be seen as a consequence of the eventual repression of the reformatory tendencies of the late sixties and early seventies in politics as well as educational and social policies. Under the increasingly conservative West German government headed by the Social Liberal Party (SPD) and later by the conservative Christian Democrats (CDU), the anterior movements for democracy fizzled out. Walser responds to this in his collection of quatrains *Der Grund zur Freude* (1978; The Reason for Joy), incisively ridiculing the political stagnation of the seventies.³⁰ With a new artistic

---

[29] Peter André Bloch, et al., "Interview mit Martin Walser," *Gegenwartsliteratur: Mittel und Bedingungen ihrer Produktion*, ed. P. A. Bloch (Bern and Munich: Francke, 1975) 259.

[30] See particularly quatrain 25 and 72, as well as those entitled "Tendenzwende" (# 73) [changing times], "Berufsverbot" (# 74) [professional censure], and "Die sanften Siebziger" (# 81) [the peaceful seventies]. Walser's essays up until 1973 echo the social critical content of his early novels more perspicaciously. In the collections *Erfahrungen und Leseerfahrungen* (1965; Experiences and Reading Experiences), *Heimatkunde* (1968; Local History), and *Wie und wovon handelt Literatur* (1973; Themes and Manners of Literature) Walser speaks at length about politics, society, and literature with the intent to sensitize the average citizen's political consciousness. Notably in "Heimatbedingungen" (1972; Prerequisites for a Homeland) Walser again calls attention to the fact that the self-centered attitudes of a relatively small number of capitalists paralyses the democratic movement in the Federal Republic. The prerequisites for a socialist democracy — the most essential "Heimatbedingung" — are stated in West Germany's constitution, and unless taken seriously, the Federal Republic can never become a real homeland for its citizens, especially those of the lower classes.

as well as a slightly modified theoretical approach, a new narrative phase of Walser crystallizes after 1975.

2

Walser's Post-1973 Narrative Phase In Context

Walser's Literary Commitment of the Seventies

IN HIS EARLY NOVELS Walser portrays individuals whose spontaneous potential is curtailed by social reality. This theme of dependency and oppression is prevalent both in his novels and novellas after 1973. As Walser considers himself a chronicler of everyday life, the thematics of his texts originate in current sociopolitical issues. Walser never addresses these issues explicitly in his fictions, but rather draws the reader's attention to them by showing their pernicious effects on average citizens among whom he includes himself. In 1980 Walser summarized the theme in his most recent novels:

> Ich habe 1976 *Jenseits der Liebe* gebracht, das ist ... die Konkurrenz zweier Angestellten unter einem Chef. Dann kam 78 das *Fliehende Pferd*, das ist die Konkurrenz zweier Männer vor zwei Frauen. Dann *Seelenarbeit*, das ist Abhängigkeit eines Angestellten von diesem Chef. Und jetzt *Schwanenhaus*, die Konkurrenz nicht von Angestellten, sondern von mittelständischen Kleinunternehmern, Geschäftsleuten.[1]

> [In 1976 I wrote "Beyond All Love," which presents ... two employees in competition before their boss. Then, in 1978, came *Runaway Horse*, which shows two men competing before two women. Then *The Inner Man*, which presents an employee's dependency on his boss. And now *The Swan Villa*, where competition occurs not among employees but rather among small-time, middle-class entrepreneurs and businessmen.]

Competition and dependency, experiences that obstruct the individual's efforts to achieve personal autonomy, move again into the foreground in Walser's prose

---

[1] Roland Lang, "Wie tief sitzt der Tick, gegen die Bank zu spielen? Interview mit Martin Walser," *Martin Walser*, ed. Klaus Siblewski (Frankfurt/M.: Suhrkamp, 1981) 56.

texts since 1980, particularly in the sequel to *Jenseits der Liebe*, the 1982 novel *Brief an Lord Liszt*. Yet the roots for these thematics in Walser's work date back several decades. Upon returning from his first extended stay in the United States in 1959 Walser felt daunted by the

> Erlebnis des Gefangenseins auf einem Kontinent, in einem Land, einer Familie, einer Sprache, dieses Abgegrenzt- und Abgekapselt- und Abgepacktsein in einer Biographie, aus der Ahnung, du bist der und der, und der hat wieder da und da unter der und der Adresse mit seinem Paß sich einzufinden. Das schien mir unerträglich.[2]

> [feeling of being held prisoner on a continent, in a country, in a family, in a language; a feeling of being confined, isolated, and wrapped up in your biography through the notion that you are supposed to be a certain someone, and that someone has to report to that particular place and address with his passport. This seemed unbearable to me.]

On the one hand the experience of being controlled manifests itself for Walser not only through social forces but also, on a more existential level, through cognitive and linguistic faculties. On the other, it permeates the private sector and affects one's self-esteem and self-identity. Walser equates this feeling of captivity with an incomplete, deficient sense of self. At that time Walser reacted to his feelings of discontent by writing the novel he entitled *Halbzeit*, drawing up, as it were, the balance sheet of half a lifetime. *Seelenarbeit* also resulted from a personal experience of this kind, where it was presumably medical treatment that instilled in Walser the impression of being dependent on or dominated by external forces. Although in this case, the dependency experienced by the author had a medical rather than a societal origin, but its intensity led Walser to proclaim that the worst possible experience is "Abhängigkeit" [dependency].[3]

Between 1974 and 1978 Walser penned the essays compiled in the volume *Wer ist ein Schriftsteller* (1979). Walser here elaborates on his concept of writing, a concept that he seems to have modified slightly in that the socio-political vocabulary of his earlier essays has yielded to a more socio-psychological line of argument. In the title piece of this collection (1974), Walser maintains that since

---

[2]Monika Totten, "Ein Gespräch mit Martin Walser in Neuengland," *Martin Walser*, ed. Klaus Siblewski, (Frankfurt/M: Suhrkamp, 1981) 28.

[3]Totten, pp. 28-29; see also Martin Walser, "Über den Umgang mit Literatur," *Martin Walser: International Perspectives*, ed. Jürgen E. Schlunk and Armand E. Singer, American University Studies, Series I, Germanic Languages and Literature 64 (New York: Lang, 1987) 206.

the writer's identity is always subjected to social influences, it can never gain stability, but is bound to remain self-conscious, insecure, and questionable. Assuming that socially disadvantaged lower-class families do not possess the requisite self-esteem and confidence to endow their children with a rigorous and unyielding sense of self, Walser draws the inference that most writers emerge from the lower strata of society (WS 37). This conclusion arises from his belief that writing serves as a therapeutic means for the writer to consolidate his unstable identity (WS 40). Writing, Walser posits, is a response to negative, oftentimes intolerable, involuntary experiences, and only in this capacity can writing question the validity and legitimacy of the extant social conditions. The writer, then, defuses the intolerability of his experiences by giving vent to an existential urge to write. Walser's understanding of realism is based on this causality. Realistic writing, he argues, requires a motive that cannot originate in literature but in reality.[4]

As the consequence of these postulates Walser advocates the critical transformation of reality into fiction. The literary product, however, is not simply a mirror of reality, but rather a critical *Auseinandersetzung* [coming to grips] with it and a salve to specific wounds inflicted on the individual by the given conditions. Thus author and reader alike are proffered new experiential and evaluative possibilities, consummating the author's ambition to empower his fictional creations with the ability to serve as an evocative test of reality (WS 16). In contrast to the 'poet' (*Dichter*) who seeks contentment in the literary licking of his wounds, the 'realistic writer' (*Schreiber*) attempts to discover the cause of these wounds. Hence Walser considers writing to be a battle against that which inflicts damage, in fact, no less than the dialectical movement from suffering to resistance (WS 41).

During the sixties, Walser regarded literature as one potential means to help clear the path to democracy and, quite apparently, assigned a concrete public function to literature. By the same token Walser always considered fiction the author's response to personal experiences — experiences, however, that are related to a broader social problem area. The necessity of social change remains the central issue in Walser's essays. In the title piece of the collection *Wie und wovon handelt Literatur* (1972), Walser demands of each author that he insure the social function of literature by means of a critical, by which he means realistic,

---

[4]Walser, "Über den Leser — soviel man in einem Festzelt darüber sagen soll" (WW 122); cf. also Ursula Reinhold, "Erfahrung und Realismus: Über Martin Walser," *Weimarer Beiträge* 21.7 (1975): 99.

portrayal of negative social conditions (WW 123). In a fervent declaration of 1968 Walser had insisted that the adequate tone of literary expression constitute itself as a "demokratische, mythenzerstörende, mutmachende Schreibe, in der sich der demokratische Befreiungsprozeß manifestiert" [democratic, encouraging, myth-shattering kind of writing that in itself expresses the process of democratic liberation].[5] Such resolute statements yielded Walser the reputation of a leftist intellectual, despite the fact that this extreme leftist propensity does not speak through his novels. For Walser the function of a novel is undoubtedly not identical to that of a political manifesto. It is rather an artistic-compository enterprise and as such — for author and reader alike — an "Entdeckungsfahrt" [expedition] (WW 136) into the reality of fiction. In Walser's novels a leftist tendency manifests itself not explicitly in specific episodes, but implicitly through the totality of the (multi-volume) work.

The pronounced political activism documented in Walser's early essays parallels the turn toward the left in the literature of the sixties. This movement was heralded by such slogans as 'emancipation' and 'self-determination,' aiming at social change.[6] When in the late sixties the leftist aspirations that culminated in the student movement of 1968 were subdued by the *Radikalenerlaß*, a decree that banned members of so-called radical organizations from occupying public positions, and the desired changes remained unrealized, Hans Magnus Enzensberger immediately denounced literature as useless, revolutionary gesticulation.[7] It was the writer Dieter Wellershoff who then, in an immediate reaction to Enzensberger, advocated a more moderated and unassuming concept of literature. As early as 1969 he anticipated the literary trend from public to private life that was to dominate subsequent decades. When literature illustrates individual suffering as a consequence of social mechanisms, Wellershoff proclaimed, it fulfills its critical potential in that it reveals the price that is often extorted by given circumstances.[8]

This kind of poetics no longer insists on the public function of literature; rather, it stresses the communicative aspect in its personal appeal to the reader. When the reader discovers an affinity to the literary protagonists' afflictions and is able to descry their social origin, he or she may develop a critical social

---

[5]"Mythen, Milch und Mut," *Christ und Welt* 18 Oct. 1968: 17.

[6]Helmut Kreuzer, "Zur Literatur der siebziger Jahre in der Bundesrepublik," *Basis* 8 (1978): 9.

[7]"Gemeinplätze, die Neueste Literatur betreffend," *Kursbuch* 15 (1968): 195.

[8]Dieter Wellershoff, *Literatur und Veränderung* (Cologne: Kiepenheuer & Witsch, 1969) 43.

consciousness. In the early seventies, Walser, who had always been an advocate of this literary concept, begins to stress the text's interaction with the reader even more forcibly. Although he still firmly believes that the literary product should reflect the historical conditions under which it was created, he now renounces the social or political function, the *Indienstnahme* of literature. In his view, literature achieves its social function through the writer's very motivation to produce it. Constituting the writer's response to personal experience caused by external factors, literature, Walser thinks, mirrors the underlying social conflicts of its very existence. Still, his pointing out that it is unreasonable to expect immediate social changes seems needless, and his statements as to a potential effect of literature are rather vague. Walser mentions the "organisierende Kraft" [activist momentum] imparted to the reader by the reader's own imitation of the author's dialectical change of perspective, yet the explicit significance of this momentum remains undefined, defying the attempt to categorize, and thus exploit it. The only concrete factor posited by Walser is his somewhat simplistic view that the act of reading is analogous to the act of writing (WW 135).[9] He thus places his trust in the reader, perhaps to disengage himself from public expectations.

In hopes of inducing the reader into an identification with his fictionalized personal experiences, Walser attempts to open a new perspective, one that will question the average citizen's conformist attitudes. He is nevertheless aware that there is no concrete proof as to a potential impact on or change in the reader. Therefore Walser refuses to address the author-reader correlation further and limits his statements to the simple declaration that a writer is someone who undergoes change through his writing (WS 42). Although Walser's demonstration of insidious facets of the given social conditions is limited to the subjective perception of his protagonists, the nexus between personal affliction and social reality becomes apparent. Eventually, however, it is the reader's response which realizes the "Protestkraft, Kritikkraft, Wunschkraft" (WS 95) [potential of protest, critique, and desire] of fiction. Walser emphasizes this in a television interview of 1985:

---

[9]This analogy marks the starting point of various reception theories. See especially George Poulet who writes at the outset of his phenomenological analysis of the act of reading: "This *I* who thinks in me when I read a book, is the *I* of the one who writes the book... As he makes us read it, he awakens in us the analogue of what he thought or felt"; "Phenomenology of Reading," *New Literary History* 1 (1969): 57. Similarly, Wolfgang Iser states that the text is brought to life through the act of concretization; "Der Lesevorgang," *Rezeptionsästhetik*, 1975, ed. Rainer Warning (Munich: Fink, 1979) 153.

> Ich kann die gesellschaftliche Dimension, die sogenannte politische Brauchbarkeit oder überhaupt gesellschaftliche Brauchbarkeit, die kann ich nicht beabsichtigen. Aber ich kann auf meine Erfahrungen, auf meine negativen Erfahrungen nach meiner Art literarisch antworten und muß dann hoffen, daß in meine negativen Erfahrungen etwas eingegangen sei, was verallgemeinerungsfähig für den Leser, der ähnliche Erfahrungen hat, ist.[10]
>
> [I cannot intend the societal dimension, the so-called political function, or societal function in general. What I *can* do, however, is to react to my negative experiences in my own literary fashion, and then I can only hope that my negative experiences contain something, which for the reader who has undergone similar experiences assumes a more general relevance.]

It is precisely these negative experiences that lead to the feeling of vulnerability, hence an incomplete and unsatisfactory self-identity. Walser is at pains to emphasize that this state of general discontent motivates him to write,[11] explicitly stating that his literary protagonists are attempts to come to terms with an autobiographical lack.[12] Although the conflicts Walser depicts in his novels are based on, or at least related to personal experience, the source of these conflicts is not subjective. The lack of self-confidence and self-identity perceived by his characters is always the consequence of external, that is, societal, manipulative influences. Since the author himself is a product of social forces, so, too, are his literary products.[13] In this manner, the self-defensive strategies of

---

[10]*Martin Walser im Gespräch mit Günter Gaus,* Television Interview with Martin Walser, ARD, NDR 2 Nov. 1985.

[11]See Martin Walser, *Wer ist ein Schriftsteller,* p. 37; *Wie und wovon handelt Literatur,* p. 123; "Rascher Überblick über unser Vermögen," *Basis* 5 (1975): 132-33; Anton Kaes, "Porträt Martin Walser. Ein Gespräch," *German Quarterly* 57 (1984): 435; Irmela Schneider, "Ansprüche an die Romanform: Ein Gespräch mit Martin Walser," *Die Rolle des Autors: Analysen und Gespräche,* ed. Irmela Schneider, Literaturwissenschaft — Gesellschaftswissenschaft 56 (Stuttgart: Klett, 1981) 103; Peter André Bloch, et. al., "Interview mit Martin Walser," *Gegenwartsliteratur: Mittel und Bedingungen ihrer Produktion,* ed. P. A. Bloch (Bern and Munich: Francke, 1975) 262; Ulrike Hick, Interview mit Martin Walser, *Martin Walsers Prosa: Möglichkeiten des zeitgenössischen Romans unter Berücksichtigung des Realismusanspruchs,* Stuttgarter Arbeiten zur Germanistik 126, ed. Ulrich Müller, et. al. (Stuttgart: Akademischer Verlag Hans-Dieter Heinz, 1983) 292-94.

[12]Kaes, p. 435.

[13]Walser, "Ein Blick durchs umgekehrte Fernrohr," Preface, *Gesellschaftspolitische Aspekte in Martin Walsers Kristlein-Trilogie,* by Heike Doane (Bonn: Bouvier, 1978) 1. See also Klaus Siblewski, "Martin Walser," *Kritisches Lexikon zur deutschsprachigen Gegenwartsliteratur,* ed. Heinz Ludwig Arnold (Munich: Text + Kritik, 1980) 2.

his protagonists assert Walser's own rebellion against such negativity as constitutes his personal experience, in effect, a rebellion by literary proxy.[14]

Departing from a subjective vantage point, Walser's narrative approach seeks to invade extra-subjective territory.[15] This literary concept, which seems to content itself with a rather modest objective, is characteristic of German literature of the seventies. It was not the declared goal of this literature to function as a vehicle for social change, but to challenge the perceptions of the individual. This tendency marks the transition from the global, socio-political criticism of the literature of the sixties to a less agitative literature of the subsequent decades. Notwithstanding the renunciation of its public function, this literature assumes its social dimension through the reader's participation. The fact that experiential knowledge has become essential for this sort of literary commitment should not be mistaken for self-sufficient escapism. Walser himself rigidly rejects the self-complacent and ahistorical narcissism of the works of the so-called New Subjectivists, although, notably with his later novels *Brandung* and *Jagd* in which the lack of societal relevance prevails, he clearly abandons this position.

Heinz Ludwig Arnold (Munich: Text + Kritik, 1980) 2.

[13]Kaes, p. 436.

[15]Thomas Nolden, "Der Schriftsteller als Literaturkritiker: Ein Porträt Martin Walsers," *Martin Walser: International Perspectives*, p. 181.

The Literary Context: Examples of New Subjectivity

THE LITERARY MOVEMENT that began to develop in West Germany during the early seventies after the revolutionary spirit of the sixties had spent its force commonly bears the label New Subjectivity (*Neue Subjektivität*). The works it has brought forth evidence the gradual abdication of explicit political themes while displaying the simultaneous rediscovery of innermost human concerns. For this reason this literature became also known as New Sensibility. Some of the most prominent and widely read authors who emerged from that post-war generation include Peter Handke, often seen as epitomizing that movement, Botho Strauß, Nicolas Born, Peter Härtling, and Bernward Vesper. In addition various established authors, among them Elias Canetti, Max Frisch, or Thomas Bernhard, contributed with their autobiographical sketches to the rapidly revitalizing psychological concerns of literature.

Its hallmarks, generally considered Peter Schneider's narrative *Lenz* and Karin Struck's first novel *Klassenliebe* (Class Love), both appeared in 1973, marking the year of transition. In *Lenz*, the protagonist's search for a political stance is interwoven with his personal quest for self-identity, while the portrayal of his emotions is not subordinated to that of external reality. In Struck's novel the quasi-autobiographical, first-person narrator displays an unusually radical openness in revealing her most secret feelings. Thematically *Klassenliebe* illustrates socio-political reality, more precisely, the narrator's social dilemma as she is climbing the social ladder. The brash discussion of decidedly political themes is supercharged with emotionalism and is also tightly connected with the purpose of self-portrayal and self-denudation with the ultimate objective of individual self-definition. Writing becomes a means for the conjuration of self (209). Formally the novel which consists of diary-like entries is characteristic of New Subjective prose.

While in the literature of the sixties there prevailed a broad, panoramic view of society, the literary production of the following decades was determined by a rather narrow angle, focusing on the conflict between individuals and society. Schneider's protagonist is considered a key figure in the literary transition to personal themes, because his emotions are no longer subordinated to political issues. Yet while in *Lenz* a distinct coexistence of personal and political themes prevails, the societal perspective in most of the subsequent New Subjective works is at best implied. For Gregor Keuschnig, the protagonist in Peter Handke's *Stunde der wahren Empfindung* (1975; *A Moment of True Feeling*, 1977), for example, all social values become suddenly meaningless as he finds himself in an identity crisis. All substance in Handke's narrative is the inner world of the protagonist. On account of this exclusively subjective point of view, any potential reasons or motives for Keuschnig's alienation remain rather vague. There are, however, indications that job-related factors may serve as a explanation. His life is ruled by a feeling of isolation and disorientation. What Handke illustrates in *Stunde der wahren Empfindung* is the individual's experience of total estrangement from external reality, but also his eventual rediscovery of a new perception of reality. The same theme is central to Handke's novel *Chinese des Schmerzes* (Chinaman of Sorrow) of 1983. In this narrative the first-person narrator Andreas Loser (a pun on its English meaning may be intended) drops out of his bourgeois profession as teacher of ancient languages, finding himself in a state of passive isolation. Again it is this loss of social context that constitutes the precondition for his ultimate achievement of a new sense of perception.

In Nicolas Born's novel *Die erdabgewandte Seite der Geschichte* (1976; The Far Side of History) the narrator describes his own identity crisis. His awareness of an inimical world that resists all comprehension causes him to withdraw from history into his own, self-composed story. Like his counterpart Keuschnig, who suddenly finds himself face to face with a nonsensical and incoherent reality, Born's narrator turns his back on the system. But even in his private sphere there arise nothing but conflicts which overshadow his relationships with his wife, his girlfriend and his best friend. Looming above, however, is his loss of orientation, the loss of a healthy symbiosis with a peacefully progressing society (20). Similar to Handke, individual isolation and the feeling of disorientation form the central theme in Born's novel. Born's narrator is possessed by the notion that his life is sliding away from under him (21). Instead of history he experiences "bloß Geschichten" (20) [merely stories], stories that resist comprehension and closure. The realization of his own insignificance as a part of the system leads him to a "Flucht in die Innerlichkeit" [withdrawal into himself] as a reaction to his "Gefangenschaft in der Äußerlichkeit" (51) [imprisonment in external reality]. Analogous to Gregor Keuschnig, who craves a job that produces something definitive and irreversible (161), Born's narrator envisions his salvation from a meaningless existence through "eine Arbeit, die einfach getan werden muß" (16) [a job that simply has to be done]. Only on the basis of his individual usefulness could he develop a new sense of social values.

An all-embracing indictment of society appears to be the concern of Thomas Bernhard's short novels *Die Ursache* (1975; "An Indication of the Cause," 1985), *Der Keller* (1976; "The Cellar: An Escape," 1985), *Der Atem* (1978; "Breath: A Decision," 1985), *Die Kälte* (1981; "In the Cold," 1985), and *Ein Kind* (1982; "A Child," 1985).[16] These texts are conceived as quasi-autobiographical sequels through which the author-narrator relates fragments of his childhood and youth. Looking back in vengeful anger, his cold, self-distancing, and non-palliative report settles scores with the past. In *Die Ursache* Bernhard illustrates the experiences of a thirteen-year-old school boy during the war and post-war period. The narrator considers himself a victim of a brutal environment that kept him an unprotected and defenseless prisoner. A pronounced historical criticism becomes repeatedly audible in the narrator's remarks about the post-war Catholic regime that presumably superseded Nazi fascism. Both ideologies, he is convinced, represent the same "menschenfeindlichen Züchtigungsmechanismus" (108) [barbarous ritual of castigation]. Furthermore federal institutions, such as the school system, are stigmatized as a "katastrophale Verstümmelungsmaschinerie" (119) [disastrous apparatus for the mutilation of the mind].

In *Der Keller* Bernhard indicts the destructive mechanisms of a society that harshly suppresses the individual's search for personal fulfillment and instead leaves him with the feeling of desperate imprisonment. The narrator's crisis comes to a dramatic climax in the following two texts. In *Der Atem* the setting is a hospital where the narrator finds himself among scores of moribund patients. Yet, although the illness of the meanwhile eighteen-year-old has reached a life-threatening stage, he tells us in *Die Kälte* that he managed to escape from the "perversen medizinischen Unheilsmühle" (148) [perverted medical disaster mill] and rediscover his determination to live. He thus wins the struggle for self-assertion, a victory, however, of so modest an objective as the mere wish to survive. As the narrator already admits in *Der Atem*, the pursuit of that goal merely insures a prolongation of the "lebenslänglichen Sterbeprozeß" (81) [life-long process of dying]. This bleak view invalidates even the last remaining ground for existential self-determination. Life itself is the penitentiary to which everyone is committed by birth. The "gesellschaftspolitische Perversität" (127)

---

[16]Although Bernhard's narratives are available in translation in the volume *Gathering Evidence. A Memoir*, trans. David McLintock (New York: Knopf, 1985), the English renditions of quotations are my own.

[socio-political perversity] of society's institutions leads the individual to the realization of his invariable existential captivity. Never does Bernhard's pessimistic portrayal of human existence attempt to address or investigate social issues, it simply condemns an abominable system.

The texts addressed display a trait typical of the New Subjective literature. While the social critical novels of the sixties, for example the novels of Böll, Grass, Lenz, or Walser, presented their protagonists as victims of the demands and promises made by society, they also pointed to the weaknesses and inadequacies of these characters. The New Subjective works, however, unquestionably acquit the individual summarily, while exclusive blame is put on an inhumane society.[17] Bernhard's objective, then, is one of self-justification, which allows him at the same time to externalize his frustrations. For this purpose, as he states in *Der Keller*, writing becomes a "Lebensnotwendigkeit" (45) [existential necessity].

Bernhard's texts are characteristic of many works of the seventies that are considered quasi-autobiographies, because their authors display a highly subjective attitude:

[E]r begnügt sich mit einer splitterhaften Darstellung seines Lebens, er bleibt dort stehen, wo er psychisch nicht mehr weiter kann; liefert Momentaufnahmen und dokumentiert seine Ehrlichkeit, indem er bewußt oder unbewußt auf seine Ängste hinweist. Dabei rückt die Autobiographie in den Bereich der schöngeistigen Literatur, und die Fiktionalisierung wird oft genug zum integralen Element der Selbstdarstellung.[18]

[He contents himself with a fragmentary portrayal of his own life and stops where he cannot go any further mentally. He presents momentary glimpses and documents his honesty by consciously or unconsciously admitting to his fears. Autobiography here approaches the realm of *belles lettres*, and in many cases fictionalization becomes an integral element of self-portrayal.]

This verdict also applies to the autobiographical fictions of Max Frisch and Peter Härtling. In his diary-like novel *Montauk* (1975; 1976) Frisch identifies himself as the narrator, who is set on self-analysis. Deliberately ignoring social issues,

---

[17]Helmut Koopmann, "Tendenzen des deutschen Romans der siebziger Jahre," *Handbuch des deutschen Romans*, ed. Helmut Koopmann (Düsseldorf: Bagel, 1983) 580.

[18]David Bronsen, "Autobiographien der siebziger Jahre: Berühmte Schriftsteller befragen ihre Vergangenheit," *Deutsche Literatur der Bundesrepublik seit 1965*, ed. Paul Michael Lützeler and Egon Schwarz (Königstein: Athenäum, 1980) 213.

Frisch hopes that his radical self-denudations will permit him a cool distance from his past and allow him to come to terms with personal problems. Mindful exclusively of his own feelings — "ICH BIN ES, DEN ICH DARSTELLE" ["IT IS MYSELF THAT I PORTRAY"] the motto reads — he seeks self-assurance both as a writer and his role as a man, downright rejecting the once respected public as a communicative partner.[19]

Peter Härtling, in his novel *Nachgetragene Liebe* (1980; In Retrospect, With Love), likewise undertakes a journey into the past by means of writing. The author-narrator recapitulates the crucial years of his childhood that determined his ambivalent relationship with his — meanwhile deceased — father, desperately trying to disclose the reasons for his father's painful lack of affection. At the same time the narrator seeks self-justification by shedding light on this unbeneficial relationship. Fully cognizant of the writing process, he resurrects the past and simultaneously assumes a more objective distance from himself. As in Frisch's case, the retrospective clarification of formative influences finally leads to self-analysis and self-definition.

Richard Schroubek, the first-person narrator in Botho Strauß's *Die Widmung* (1977; *Devotion*, 1979), is disgusted with society's blunt deceptions and withdraws into himself in order to engage in "Ich-Forschung" (41) ["self-analysis"; 32]. Like the narrator in Born's novel, Schroubek is unnerved and bedazzled by society, which has left him politically disoriented. The traceless disappearance of his girlfriend leaves him further emotionally unsettled. In an effort to come to a closer understanding of his emotions and gain a new sense of self he begins to compile the "Biografie seiner leeren Stunden" (127) ["biography of his empty hours"; *Devotion* 105].

All texts discussed here investigate troubled relationships between an individual and external reality, most allowing this individual to function as the narrator of his story. The emphasis clearly lies on the subjective-emotional equipoise of the narrator while external conditions are either excluded or — as in Bernhard's works — globally denounced. Disillusionment, anger, pessimism, and fear are the motives for these protagonists to retreat into subjective reality, accounting for the lack of a social critical perspective. It is the personal concern of these author-narrators to reveal the ontological causes for their vexing self-doubts and insecurities. This sort of self-reflection seeks to stabilize their

---

[19]Cf. Frisch's 1958 essay "Öffentlichkeit als Partner," *Gesammelte Werke in zeitlicher Folge 7*, ed. Hans Mayer (Frankfurt/M.: Suhrkamp, 1976) 244-52, where Frisch voices the opposite view, namely that he writes exclusively for his readers.

shattered psychological make-up. In the New Subjective works the individual functions both as the means and the objective of narration.[20] The individual describes, portrays, and analyzes himself because everything external to him resists depiction, portrayal, and analysis for want of a logical coherence. One could argue, then, that it is indeed the abstract system of society that is implicated and held responsible for the deformations of the individual. Since this system is no longer depictable and poses a monstrous threat to the individual, it necessitates his retreat into subjectivity. Walser too employs his protagonists as figural media eluding social reality by barricading themselves within their thoughts and emotions. Yet the goal of his novels is not a narcissistic self-presentation — neither of the author nor of the protagonist. It is Walser's intent to unveil the adverse social conditions and their effect on his protagonists, an intent that manifests itself in his narrative approach.

---

[20]Linda C. DeMeritt, *New Subjectivity and Prose Forms of Alienation: Peter Handke and Botho Strauß*, Studies in Modern German Literature 5 (New York: Lang, 1987) 8.

The Narrative Perspective

THE INTROJECTION OF the thematics in Walser's novels after 1975 has its formal basis in the modified narrative perspective. While Walser presents his narratives now in the third person, the narrative perspective is still centered in the character's consciousness. An outside narrator is not noticeable, yet the use of the third person and of the simple past point to a mediating narrative voice. Oftentimes the narratives are carried by narrated monologue, a form of figural narration that stands between direct and indirect speech and expresses the thoughts of the character — contrary to the interior monologue — in the third person.[21] Thus narrated monologue casts "the language of a subjective mind into the grammar of objective narration." While formally it points to the presence of an implied narrator, it is this narrator's "*identification* — but not his *identity* — with the character's mentality that is supremely enhanced by this technique."[22] This kind of narration renounces *ex cathedra* statements of an omniscient narrator and instead mediates external reality via the consciousness of the perceiving character. This creates the illusion of immediacy, the suspension in an instant present and makes possible a high degree of dramatic and mimetic representation of external as well as internal events, including the penetration of the subliminal zones of the mind.[23] This, then, entails a process of identification between reader and character, and the reader is invited to meet the character with empathy and benevolence.

As it is the protagonist's consciousness that is mediated, albeit in the third person, it is often almost impossible for the reader to note the presence of a potential outside narrator. On the other hand a narrative voice implies itself through the use of the third person and the simple past. This co-existence of

---

[21]For a most lucid explication of narrated monologue see Dorrit Cohn, *Transparent Minds: Narrative Modes for Presenting Consciousness in Fiction* (Princeton: Princeton UP, 1978) 99-140.

[22]Cohn, pp. 117, 112.

[23]Stanzel, *Theorie des Erzählens* (Göttingen: Vandenhoeck & Ruprecht, 1979) 246; see also Cohn, p. 126.

character and implied narrator (who share the same perspective, but speak in different voices)[24] creates a tension between the two. Walser handles this tension skilfully and uses it for sudden and subtle changes of perspective. This is achieved through the shift from past tense to present tense discourse as for example in *Brandung*: "Unter diesem Himmel hatte man sich also den Pazifik zu denken.... Dieser Anblick sprengt ihm schier sein sogenanntes Fassungsvermögen" (B 29).[25] This time shift immediately stops the flow of the narrated monologue and questions the subjective mediation through the figural medium, that is, the character. In this vein the point of view of an implied narrator often but almost imperceptibly disrupts or blends into the protagonist's perspective in order to subtly comment on, ironize, or simply objectify certain thoughts, statements or actions. It immediately takes the reader out of the temporal and spatial context experienced by the character and discontinues his or her identification with the character. Whereas the reader is encouraged by the narrated monologue to share the character's perspective, he or she is now invited or even forced to share the perspective of the implied narrator's commenting voice. The present tense clearly evokes a more ironic distance of the implied narrator from the character.[26]

Except for *Brief an Lord Liszt*, which as an epistolary novel is written in the first person, Walser usually avoids the use of the first person pronoun. Instead, the narration switches to second person discourse, which may be interpreted as the narrator addressing his character or the character addressing himself. In *Jagd* one reads: "Er hatte es satt, der zu sein, der er zu sein hatte. Geh hin und lang dem eine ..." (J 96) [He was fed up with the idea of being the way he was expected to be. Go up to him and slap him ...]. In the following example from *Ein fliehendes Pferd* personal pronouns change within the same sentence: "Wehe dir Sabine, wenn er nur vier Bände schafft" (FP 11) ["And may the Lord have mercy on you, Sabina, if he only gets through four" (volumes of Kierkegaard's

---

[24]In certain instances, however, there occurs even a fusion of narrative voices, a so-called "stylistic contagion," when the reporting syntax is maintained, but the diction seems to reflect the character's own thoughts or words; see Cohn, p. 33.

[25]This time shift is not accounted for in the English translation: "And under this sky was, one knew, the Pacific.... The sight seemed almost to burst the bounds of his emotional grasp" (Br 28).

[26]The narrative ambiguity resulting from the shift from narrated monologue to the present tense is discussed perceptively by Jean-Maurice Martin, *Untersuchungen zum Problem der Erlebten Rede. Der ursächliche Kontext der Erlebten Rede, dargestellt an Romanen Robert Walsers*, Europäische Hochschulschriften, Series I, Deutsche Sprache und Literatur 1009 (Bern: Lang, 1987) 125-26.

diaries); RH 2]. In such cases the narrating and the figural voice seem to fuse as the narrated monologue temporarily blends into interior monologue and the implied narrator disappears completely behind the character. Rarely does one encounter statements in the interior monologue, such as "Ja, ich suche ein Schlupfloch" (JL 155) [Yes, so I am looking for a retreat], a mental utterance by Franz Horn in *Jenseits der Liebe*. Gottlieb Zürn in *Jagd* seems to be the only protagonist whom Walser has granted frequent permission to voice his thoughts directly. More typical are passages of indirect style, reported speech or thought, where the mediation through an implied narrator on which the character is dependent is clearly visible. Yet, here too, the narrative voice invariably adopts the protagonist's angle of vision and yields to the figural thoughts, effacing once again the demarcation between the narrator's and the character's linguistic idiom, so that what is reported seems to be identical with the character's self-knowledge. Given the lack of evaluative judgments, the implied narrator does not appear to have a cognitive privilege over the character.[27]

Only very few statements seem to reflect an omniscient point of view, for example: "Xavers Vorstellungen begannen zu rasen" (SA 254) ["Xaver's fantasies began to race"; IM 237], although even in this sentence psycho-narration is still maintained in that the figural perspective is not transcended, but rather presented through the use of verbs and nouns of consciousness. At times one finds passages of direct speech by other characters which, by virtue of the absence of quotation marks, must be read as filtered through the protagonist's mind.[28] The hidden, yet permanent presence of an outside narrator points to the limited perspective of the protagonist and prevents the reader from taking the character all too readily at his word. While the character's autonomy in his function as a figural medium is sustained, his subjective perspective is at the same time undermined by the presence of an implied narrator, whose true identity is veiled. This play with perspectives reflects an essential component of the texts' thematic structure, namely the protagonists' pathological urge to camouflage *their* true identities. In *Brandung* we read:

> Man weiß nie, ob man sich wirklich durchschaut, wenn man sich ganz zu durchschauen glaubt. Vielleicht fällt man nur auf eine weitere Kulisse herein, die man vor den wirklichen Befund schiebt, weil der für das sogenannte Selbstgefühl unerträglich wäre. (B 13)

---

[27]Cohn has termed this the "consonant type of psycho-narration [that] displays disparity of values even less than disparity of knowledge [between narrator and character]" (32).

[28]Cohn uses the term "unsignaled quoted monologue" (111).

[We never know whether we understand our real motive when we believe we do understand our real motive. Perhaps we are merely deceived by a different backdrop that we have shifted in front of the true scenario because the latter would be intolerable for our so-called self-perception. Br 8]

Here, Helmut Halm (or rather the implied narrator who mediates his perspective) expresses doubts about the objectivity of self-knowledge and of human perception in general. The entire novel is carried by a nostalgic, almost bitter tone as the character finds himself in an existential crisis owing to his realization of the deceptions of life and the illusion of reality.

The dependency on a higher narrating authority entails the psychological weakening of Walser's characters — as opposed to Walser's earlier novels, where narrative perspective and narrative voice are identical, namely unified in the hero. This illustrates the thematic shift of accent denoting the shift from a more sociological view in Walser's early prose to a distinctly psychological approach in his later works. The characters must now react to a "Gegenwelt," a counter-force that exerts a threatening pressure on them.[29] This increasing external psychological pressure brings with it the protagonists' progressive loss of self-esteem and disintegrating sense of identity. The protagonists withdraw into an introverted self-isolation in order to resist an inimical environment.

This narrative technique reflects the theme of the characters' alienation and their struggle for self-assertion. The subjective perspective makes the depiction of reality as a trustworthy totality impossible. Helmut Halm explicitly addresses the problematic of a subjective world view when he deplores that "[w]hat a person sees reflects virtually nothing of what actually *is*" (RH 64). The outside world in these texts presents itself only as perceived by the protagonists. The story unfolds not at the initiative of these protagonists, but rather follows their reactions to external, i.e. society's manipulative influences. Their (social) behavior is confined to developing defensive strategies in order to secure themselves a minimal realm of unassailability by public expectations.

---

[29]See Anton Kaes, "Porträt Martin Walser. Ein Gespräch," Interview with Martin Walser, *German Quarterly* 57 (1984): 437.

The Internalized Thematics

ASIDE FROM THE modified narrative perspective, Walser undertakes a new artistic approach to the form of his post-1973 narratives. The formal structure of these narratives reflects compository discipline and linguistic density. Gone are the days of Anselm Kristlein's loquacious digressions, and consequently the plot unravels much more economically, proceeding in a linear and purposive fashion toward an eventual climax. Furthermore, compared to the earlier novels, the scope of narrated time, setting, and external events is drastically reduced, while the focus lies on the individual protagonist's internal suffering and the impossibility of gaining relief. Owing to this narrowed point of view, other characters remain pallid and faceless. The voices of bosses and friends alike fade away, and both setting and sound of events are introjected into the protagonist's mind.[30]

With the conclusion of the trilogy Walser bids farewell to Kristlein and his social upstart mentality of the fifties and sixties. The last sentence of *Der Sturz* seems to capture the cynicism of Kristlein's lasting disillusionment. Isolated and paralyzed he will vegetate in apathy: "Es fielen jetzt Glück und Ende zusammen wie beim Biß" (S 356) [Like the closing of jaws, his happiness and his end now clashed]. It is several years before a successor emerges to evaluate Kristlein's defeatist capitulation to society's immutability, a successor who awakens to once again subject societal foibles to the light of day. When Franz Horn opens his eyes at the beginning of *Jenseits der Liebe* his teeth are clenched. It is the beginning of a new chapter of suffering, although under slightly modified auspices. From the outset the new protagonists find themselves in a state of introversion, isolated from others, and fixated on themselves and their mental misery.

---

[30]See Thomas Beckermann, "'Ich bin sehr klein geworden': Versuch über Walsers Entblößungsverbergungssprache," *Martin Walser: International Perspectives*, ed. Jürgen E. Schlunk and Armand E. Singer, American University Studies, Series 1, Germanic Languages and Literature 64 (New York: Lang, 1987) 22; also Ursula Reinhold, "Zu Walsers Romanen in den siebziger Jahren," *Tendenzen und Autoren: Zur Literatur der siebziger Jahre in der BRD* (Berlin: Dietz, 1982) 298.

In his coda to Anselm Kristlein, Walser states that Kristlein had never been happy, let alone in control of or in harmony with himself.[31] Being exposed to nothing but hostilities, the life of Kristlein, the would-be *parvenu*, was a continuous battle. Although in retrospect Walser denies his protagonist any self-confidence, he nonetheless considers him a hero, because he believed in survival. Kristlein, Walser continues, could not help but lead a life of conformity, never giving thought to the price of his life style. The debts continue to be paid by Walser's protagonists since 1976, who have long since forfeited their natural spontaneity to cope with their environment. The relationship between them and the outside world focuses on psychological ramifications and mirrors the deformations of their suffering consciousness. The protagonists of this era have internalized Kristlein's extroverted verbosity. Hence, in *Seelenarbeit*, the chauffeur Xaver Zürn engages in self-contained dialogues with his boss since he is unable to communicate through genuine conversation.

While the Kristlein novels centered on the protagonist's zealous struggle for self-realization via social ascent, the later works illustrate the characters' resignation and their exhaustion from this struggle. Despite the fact that they have moved up the social ladder, they have failed to find their yearned-for happiness and are now preoccupied with developing strategies for survival in order to come to terms with their failures. These characters are individual examples of the changing phase from the social, political, and economic euphoria of the fifties to the stagnation and recession of the seventies.[32] Undoubtedly, the protagonists of the seventies and eighties have attained higher living standards, a mechanism by which they seem to realize that throughout their laborious social ascent they "justified and absolved even the most destructive and oppressive features of th[is] enterprise."[33] Thus the recognition of their own passive contributions to social oppression renders them unwilling to participate any longer in the masquerade of seeking advancement through conformism. Aware that the system has claimed them as victims, they have become "*Unterlegenheitsspezialisten*" [experts of subordination][34] whose sole concern it is to withdraw from society.

---

[31]"Nachruf auf einen Verstummten," *Martin Walser*, ed. Klaus Siblewski (Frankfurt/M.: Suhrkamp, 1981) 54-57.

[32]Thomas Beckermann, "Entblößungsverbergungssprache," p. 20.

[33]Marcuse, *One-Dimensional Man*, p. 146.

[34]Sybille Brantl, "Martin Walser: Sein Leben spricht Bände," Interview with Martin Walser, *Cosmopolitan* (German edition) Oct. 1986: 35.

The nature of the dependencies of Walser's everyday heroes is closely related to his modified narrative approach. It is no longer the material dependence of an Anselm Kristlein which limits their possibilities. Indeed, the immediate economic pressure to which Kristlein was once exposed has vanished into a psychological pressure, which, however, can be traced to economico-political conditions. These protagonists are ruled by the need to disguise and conceal themselves as they experience a sense of captivity generated by their rampant inferiority complex toward their environment. Although these feelings of inferiority are primarily evident in their intercourse with superiors, they also manifest themselves in public as well as private behavior patterns. This assertion is of particular significance in *Ein fliehendes Pferd* and *Brandung*, where the effects of social conditioning severely encroach on as private an enterprise as leisure activities.

Franz Horn in *Jenseits der Liebe* withdraws into a self-isolation of muted suffering in order to escape the influence of his competitor Liszt, who has ousted him from a leading position. In *Ein fliehendes Pferd* Helmut Halm is confronted with society's attacks personified by the manic conformist Klaus Buch. In this novella Walser warns the reader against the threat of an anonymous societal apparatus. Yet even after *Ein fliehendes Pferd*, Walser's most celebrated work to date,[35] he felt motivated to bolster the degree to which society insinuates itself into the lives of his protagonists, altering and amplifying their sufferings.[36] Additional evidence as to the obsolescence of the conventional forms of dependence — those under which Kristlein had been suffered — can be found in the novel *Das Schwanenhaus*, where Walser grants a senior Kristlein a brief appearance. Being one of those industrial pioneers, who single-handedly built up their own corporation, his entrance is dashing and exudes self-confidence. Meanwhile, however, aged and drained of all his vitality, but enormously wealthy, his death is reported only a little later. The later protagonists clearly belong to a new generation and reflect "das Leidensprofil der Familie Kristlein ... anders" [the afflictions of the Kristlein family in a different manner].[37]

---

[35]For details on its reception see Hans Erich Struck, *Ein fliehendes Pferd*, Oldenbourg Interpretationen 27 (Munich: Oldenbourg, 1988) 79-84.

[36]See Monika Totten, "Ein Gespräch mit Martin Walser in Neuengland," *Martin Walser*, ed. Klaus Siblewski (Frankfurt/M.: Suhrkamp, 1981) 37.

[37]Roland Lang, "Wie tief sitzt der Tick, gegen die Bank zu spielen? Interview mit Martin Walser," *Martin Walser*, ed. Klaus Siblewski (Frankfurt/M.: Suhrkamp, 1981) 53.

The Petty-Bourgeois 'Hero'

WALSER'S PROTAGONISTS ARE typically drawn from the lower classes of society, more precisely, they are the descendents of blue-collar working class families. Although they have, by virtue of their personal aspirations and public education, long since attained a material and social middle-class status, they continue to cling to their inextricable emotional ties with their class of origin, which Walser loosely defines as the petty bourgeoisie, the German *Kleinbürgertum*. In his novels Walser tells "Kleinbürgergeschichte. Also die Geschichte der meisten Leute" (WS 25) [petty-bourgeois history, hence, the (hi)story of most people]. Basically Walser's petty bourgeoisie encompasses a class of average citizens who invariably derive from that segment of the social spectrum comprising the lower to lower middle class, which in his view includes not only the proletariat but also various sectors of white-collar working class, such as tenured public servants, the German *Beamtenstand*. Walser's early novels are particularly illustrative of the mania of social advancement, combined with the need for subordination and conformity which account for the discontent and psychological malaise of employees and public servants.[38]

As the lower-class individual is preoccupied with his social ascent, Walser's protagonists resemble that uniform type of employees characterized by Siegfried Kracauer as a natural selection bred under the pressure of social conditions and inevitably promoted by the economy and its appeal to the pertinent consumer needs.[39] Since this social stratum lacks a concretely defined affiliation with a specific social class, it orients itself toward the bourgeoisie. Walser calls this upward orientation the "Rette-sich-wer-kann-Praxis" (WS 28) [every-man-for-himself attitude], declaring it the goal of every petty-bourgeois citizen to convert as quickly as possible to the ruling class so as to rid himself of his innate social

---

[38]Urs Jaeggi, "Zwischen den Mühlsteinen: Der Kleinbürger oder die Angst vor der Geschichte," *Kursbuch* 45 (1976): 162.

[39]*Die Angestellten: Aus dem neuesten Deutschland*, 1930 (Frankfurt/M.: Suhrkamp, 1971) 25.

inferiority complex. By contributing his own productivity the petty-bourgeois only ensures the efficacy of the system.

In 1964 Walser complained about the shortcomings of West German literature. Although the petty-bourgeoisie may be said to be the successor to the bourgeoisie, whose rise started during the eighteenth century (EL 96), Walser feels that the petty-bourgeois has been sorely neglected in German literature. Insisting that literature contain reference to socio-historical reality, Walser demands the abolishment of pseudo-realistic literature in favor of a critical debate of contemporary issues. His works from 1957 to 1973 place special emphasis on the social mobility of his petty-bourgeois protagonists. Walser's later texts, then, stand in stark contrast to his earlier ones, preferring to investigate the characters' psychological deformations, the mechanisms to which they are exposed *after* having attained the desired bourgeois social status. Marcuse considers the social mobility of the petty-bourgeoisie the essential structural principle of an advanced industrial society. For "'the people,' previously the ferment of social change, have 'moved up' to become the ferment of social cohesion."[40] The stagnant social conditions in Walser's novels attest to that, because they show how society has replaced, in the words of Marcuse,

> personal dependence (...) with dependence on the 'objective order of things' (on economic laws, the market etc). To be sure, the 'objective order of things' is itself the result of domination, but it is nevertheless true that domination now generates a higher rationality — that of society which sustains its hierarchic structure while exploiting ever more efficiently the natural and mental resources, and distributing the benefits of this exploitation on an ever-larger scale. The limits of this rationality, and its sinister force, appear in the progressive enslavement of man by a productive apparatus which perpetuates the struggle for existence....[41]

Walser, who considers himself a petty-bourgeois citizen, regards petty-bourgeois life as a representative form of contemporary existence:

> Für mich fließt alles, was ich mir vorstellen kann, im Kleinbürgerlichen zusammen. Das kommt halt daher, weil ich selber Kleinbürger bin, kleinbürgerlich geboren und aufgewachsen. Daher können andere Klassen bei mir eher nur Gastspiele geben. Meine Arbeitshaltung kann nie eine andere

---

[40]Marcuse, *One-Dimensional Man*, p. 256.

[41]Marcuse, *One-Dimensional Man*, p. 144.

sein, als daß der Held Kleinbürger-Frequenz hat, und ich könnte keine andere anstreben.[42]

[For me everything I can imagine is a part of petty-bourgeois existence. This is simply a consequence of my own background, as I was born and grew up to be a petty-bourgeois. This is why other (social) classes can merely give guest performances in my books. When I work my heroes automatically have a petty-bourgeois wave-length, I could not design them in any other way.]

Elsewhere Walser has stated the reasons for his sympathies with the petty-bourgeois hero, who in his opinion is "eine ausgenutzte, ausgepowerte Figur ... in der Geschichte" [an exploited, washed-up figure ... in history], lacking a historical consciousness as well as collective self-esteem.[43] Another reason for Walser's genuine devotion to the petty-bourgeois hero is the general social reputation of that class. Society, Walser elaborates, has created a negative image of the petty-bourgeois with regard to his cultural taste, his intellectual standards, his political, and perhaps even his erotic preferences.[44] Walser's statements document his partisanship with the socially underprivileged, with those who are subjected to superior authorities.

Society's oppressive power mechanisms become one of the prevalent topics in Walser's most recent essays, the 1986 collection *Geständnis auf Raten* (Confession by Installments). Whoever exercises power, Walser writes, abuses it (GR 74). In most of the thirty-six short essays contained in this volume he criticizes the miscellaneous misuses of power that promote the oppression of the petty-bourgeois and hence are antagonistic to a democratic ideal.[45] In each of his novels Walser presents an individual who embodies the effects of societal manipu-

---

[42]Ursula Reinhold, "Gespräch," Interview with Martin Walser, *Tendenzen und Autoren: Zur Literatur der siebziger Jahre in der BRD* (Berlin: Dietz, 1982) 290. As for details on Walser's own background, see Anthony Waine, *Martin Walser*, pp. 7-11; furthermore Michael Winkler, "Martin Walser," *Dictionary of Literary Biography 75: Contemporary German Fiction Writers Second Series*, ed. Wolfgang D. Elfe and James Hardin, (Detroit: Gale, 1988) 243.

[43]Hans Magnus Enzensberger, "Von der Unaufhaltsamkeit des Kleinbürgertums: Eine soziologische Grille," *Kursbuch* 45 (1976): 4, 6. Enzensberger also refers to the petty-bourgeois citizen's lack of self-confidence and political influence, as well as his enthusiastic conformism and unquestioning propensity to consumerism.

[44]See Totten, p. 34.

[45]See *Geständnis auf Raten*, pp. 26, 34, 80-81, 88, 94, 104.

lation. An important aspect of his characters' psychological make-up can be derived from Walser's concept of irony as defined in his Frankfurt lectures.

Selbstbewußtsein und Ironie:
The Irony of Petty-Bourgeois Existence.

WALSER'S THEORETICAL EXPOSITIONS on self-confidence and irony, which date back to 1973, display a distinct relation and relevance to the conflicts depicted in his fictions. Analogous to the theme of Walser's novels, his concept of irony derives from the "kleinbürgerliche Bedingung" (SI 167) [petty-bourgeois premise]. This origin remains visible as Walser undertakes the development of his own concept, contrasting two principal notions of irony. One pole is represented by the classic tradition of bourgeois irony, a tradition that commences with the romantic philosopher Friedrich Schlegel (1772-1829) and his contemporary, the little known writer Adam Müller (1779-1829), and culminates in the twentieth century with Thomas Mann (1875-1955). The other pole is the petty-bourgeois variant of irony which Walser traces back to Socrates and he delineates its recurrences in Kierkegaard (1813-1855) and Hegel (1770-1831). By juxtaposing both traditions Walser decidedly distances himself from the bourgeois concept of irony. His fundamental objection is that bourgeois irony ostensibly originated in Schlegel's misinterpretation of Socrates' and Johann Gottlieb Fichte's (1762-1814) writings.

Walser's concept of irony rests upon Socrates' famous statement: I know that I know nothing, where the affirmative statement of the first clause is negated in the second. Therefore, Walser reasons, Socrates' blunt revelation of a negative state of affairs in an affirmative manner, the affirmation of his own intellectual incompetence, must inadvertently appear ironical. Walser believes that irony must be involuntary by definition, and it is by virtue of being uncontrived that it gains the property of such grave seriousness (SI 28). The serious aspect of irony in literature, then, is the consistency with which it has the protagonist uncover and acquiesce to negative conditions (e.g. I know that I know nothing). The point of it all, as Walser explains, is that the reader will discover the lack and engender "die Entbindung des Schlechten, auf daß es erscheine und dadurch auf der Strecke bleibe ..." (SI 41) [the localization of negative aspects, so that they may become visible and thus perish]. Granting unconditional legitimacy to the negative elements embedded in accepted mores allowed Socrates to identify flaws and deficiencies of external reality (SI 40).

Walser criticizes Schlegel for misinterpreting Socrates. He takes Schlegel to task for accusing Socrates of simulating a naïve exterior while concealing his true intelligence. Hence, it is Schlegel's conclusion that Socrates' irony is at the same time overt and outspoken as well as unrecognizably veiled (SI 33). In Walser's view, Schlegel undervalues Socrates' genuine concern, a concern that Walser believes to be unmistakably earnest and educational (SI 34). Schlegel, conversely, conceives of Socrates' irony as a poetic license of sorts, which allows the poet to elevate himself above both his own prejudices and the world's. Since Schlegel categorizes irony simply as self-parody (SI 34), Walser disparages, one would — if one were to agree with Schlegel — have to classify Socratic irony as bourgeois irony — an irony that merely reflects the author's sublime self-consciousness and arrogance and must not be considered a literary phenomenon (SI 107).

Like the authors of the bourgeois irony, their fictional characters — Walser cites Thomas Mann's *Tonio Kröger* (1903; 1925) as the prime example — are endowed with the self-confidence of the ruling class and exude imperturbable self-complacency (SI 111, 118). Walser rejects this bourgeois irony outright, believing it to be merely a means of self-glorification. He sees in Schlegel, Adam Müller, and especially Thomas Mann typical representatives of this tradition as all of them descended from influential bourgeois families and were, by right of birth so to speak, furnished with a firm and sound self-esteem. In Müller's writings too, Walser detects a kind of irony that in his view is replete with conceit and a sublime self-complacency. Walser traces Schlegel's as well as Müller's use of irony to their assumed bourgeois elitism, a presumptuous attitude completely detached from a concern with social conflicts.

Walser conceives of irony as the manifestation, or rather the result of a certain social class consciousness. Just as he explains bourgeois irony as originating in the unshakable self-confidence of the bourgeois author, he considers the petty-bourgeois variant a mirror of socio-psychological conditions. Walser here resorts to Fichte's thesis according to which the self becomes aware of and experiences itself *ex negativo*, that is, to the extent by which it is defined and delimited by forces external to itself, to wit, the non-self. Hence, the self-identity of an individual is entirely determined by the outside world. The greater the influence exerted by the outside world, the more difficult the experience of a genuine sense of self for the individual. Thus self-confidence or self-identity must necessarily be experienced primarily in its limitation, insufficiency or lack. Fichte's low social background gives Walser a valid reason to sympathize with

Fichte's dialectical method of deducing self-confidence from the interplay between self and outside world. He therefore extols Fichte's successful attempt to achieve an autonomous, solipsistic self, in admiration of this glorious self-liberation of a petty-bourgeois identity that had little opportunity of finding external recognition (SI 62).

If applied to the petty-bourgeois consciousness, Socrates' sentence would have to read: I know that I *am* nothing. Since the given social conditions deny the lower-class individual the accessibility of a solid sense of self, he or she can only experience self-esteem by somehow achieving a sense of harmony with the outside world. Such a state of accordance, however, can only be gained if the individual endorses the external conditions regardless of their restrictive potential, and ignores or suppresses his or her genuine desires. The continual self-denial of a literary protagonist in order to experience harmony with the outside world creates what Walser describes as ironic style (SI 178). The identities of these protagonists are negative identities, originating in the negative self-confidence of the oppressed who sacrifice their personalities to the ruling conditions, which they accept, affirm, internalize, reproduce, and consolidate. Yet, since that negative potential is all these protagonists possess, they cherish it as their sole means to realize their personalities and find happiness. A petty-bourgeois identity, then, reveals itself essentially as a non-identity or an identity of alienation.

As for the literary archetypes of this petty-bourgeois irony of subordination and self-denial, Walser admires especially Robert Walser's Jakob von Gunten in the novel of the same title (1908) and Kafka's Gregor Samsa in *Die Verwandlung* (1915; *The Metamorphosis*, 1937). Through their conscious, yet compulsive attempts to affirm the restrictive social conditions with which they are confronted, these characters endeavor to compensate for their fundamental deficiency, namely the lack of a self-assertive impetus. By euphorically exercising a conformist ritual, the petty-bourgeois protagonist becomes oblivious to society's oppressive mechanisms and invariably secures for himself a sense of congruity with the system. Walser conceives of the petty-bourgeois irony as a response to historical conditions, more precisely, to the clash of social classes.[46] Similar to the literary product, which is an outcome of the writer's reaction to onerous experiences, this irony is the consequence of the protagonist's compulsive acceptance and approval of society's demands. Yet, whereas the act of writing constitutes itself as a means to contradict social deficiencies, the subversive potential of Walser's irony is at

---

[46]Cf. Walser's statements in an interview with Peter André Bloch, *Gegenwartsliteratur: Mittel und Bedingungen ihrer Produktion*, ed. P. A. Bloch (Bern and Munich: Francke, 1975) 265.

best implied. The desperate struggle of the protagonist who suppresses himself automatically questions the legitimacy of the given conditions. Thus the reader is made aware of the oppressive potential of external reality and the lack of prospects for social change, an awareness that, so Walser hopes, will kindle the reader's desire for change.

On the one hand the ironic strategy of acquiescence and resignation to reality could be interpreted as the glorification of conformism, which, of course, would invalidate any subversive impulse of that irony. After all, Walser himself defined the petty-bourgeois as someone who is willing and proud to exploit himself and celebrate his own misery.[47] Conversely, the positive potential of petty-bourgeois irony lies in the questions it poses, questions that challenge the given conditions to justify themselves, so that in the long run, extant forms of domination may be abolished — an admittedly utopian achievement of irony that even Walser formulates only as wishful thinking.

According to Walser, every novel gives an account of the ontogenesis of a self-identity (SI 155). As Walser's protagonists are conditioned by their petty-bourgeois background, his texts are to be understood as portrayals of petty-bourgeois consciousness. As to how this concept of irony manifests itself in Walser's novels, it will be sketched within the textual analyses. It should be noted that only *Jenseits der Liebe* represents an ironical novel in Walser's sense.[48] The protagonists of Walser's other novels periodically exercise the irony of self-negation without succumbing to its inexorable consequentiality that ends with the irreversible acceptance of a negative identity.

---

[47]Ursula Reinhold, "Gespräch," Interview with Martin Walser, *Tendenzen und Autoren: Zur Literatur der siebziger Jahre in der BRD* (Berlin: Dietz, 1982) 290.

[48]Heike Doane has investigated the ironic style of that novel in her essay "Martin Walsers Ironiebegriff: Definition und Spiegelung in drei späten Prosawerken," *Monatshefte* 77 (1985): 195-212.

3

Self-Destruction of a Damaged Identity:
Jenseits der Liebe

WALSER'S FIRST NOVEL FOLLOWING the Kristlein trilogy received controversial reviews by the feuilleton press. The sparseness of scholarly responses to the novel to date is probably in part attributable to the negative verdicts espoused predominantly in national West German newspapers. While the reviewers of *Jenseits der Liebe* were not impressed with Walser's style, they further disliked the novel's subjective narrative perspective. These critics, however, neglected the author's attempt to reconcile the diction with the protagonist's state of mind.[1] Owing to the novel's subjective point of view, some critics were reluctant to ascribe a general validity to the societal problematics portrayed. An outside narrator, it was claimed, should have intervened more noticeably and commented on the main character's perceptions. Again it was overlooked that the subjective perspective is mediated and thus transcended by an implied narrator. *Jenseits der Liebe* depicts a consciousness, or more precisely: the modes of reaction of a consciousness (de)formed under certain external conditions.

The internalized plot,[2] then, illustrates the gradual self-destruction of an identity already acutely damaged by the capitalist principle of competition. The

---

[1] See summarily Ursula Bessen, "Martin Walser — *Jenseits der Liebe*: Anmerkungen zur Aufnahme des Romans bei der literarischen Kritik," *Martin Walser*, ed. Klaus Siblewski (Frankfurt/M.: Suhrkamp, 1981) 218-22.

[2] In order to distinguish between a merely temporal chain of fictional events and their causal connection, the terms 'story' and 'plot' are used here according to their definition given by E. M. Forster. 'Story,' then, denotes "a narrative of events in time sequence," whereas the 'plot' of a narrative places the emphasis on the causality of events. See *Aspects of the Novel*, 1927 (New York: Harcourt, Brace & World, 1954) 30 and 87. Forster's distinction thus differs considerably from that made by the Russian Formalist Boris Tomashevsky, whose concept of 'story' embraces both the temporal and causal sequence of events. The 'plot,' however, for Tomashevsky denotes the arrangement and thematic connection of events, it is how the reader learns the story; "Thematics," *Russian Formalist Criticism: Four Essays*, ed. Paul A. Olson, trans. Lee T. Lemon and Marion J. Reis (Lincoln: U of Nebraska Press, 1965) 66-67.

main character, forty-four-year-old Franz Horn, holds an executive position as a sales manager in a corporation that manufactures dentures, a job he has filled for seventeen years. His days, however, seem numbered when the dynamic new executive Dr. Liszt is hired, for he is soon to replace Horn in his rank. As indicated by the novel's title, Horn functions as a part of the system that has sacrificed such human values as sincerity and affection to the omnipresent pressure to perform. *Jenseits der Liebe* portrays the incompatibility of these conditions with the individual's claim to self-realization. Although the process of Horn's alienation is illuminated gradually through the use of expansive flashbacks, the narrative focuses on Horn's crippled personality as the result of this process. While the external events embrace only a few days (his trip to England, his return and subsequent suicide attempt), Horn's reflections establish a second narrative level on which crucial events in his past professional life are recapitulated, accounting for his deformed identity. Horn is thus presented as a victim of the system, one of the casualties of the self-destructive mechanisms of internalized competition. Drained of all energy to resist his ostensibly inevitable demise, Horn finds himself at an advanced stage of self-alienation. Eventually, his progressing social isolation and emotional atrophy, facilitated by his waning professional efficiency, culminate in his (unsuccessful) suicide attempt.

Horn's personal history, which is recounted retrospectively in the sequel *Brief an Lord Liszt*, is characteristic of Walser's protagonists. Like Hans Beumann in Walser's first novel, Franz Horn is born the illegitimate child of a waitress. When his mother marries a blue-collar worker notorious for his consumption of alcohol as well for his gambling habit, relatives avoid the family until the socially ungainly stepfather's early death. Notwithstanding his fondness for his stepfather, Horn can neither idolize nor identify with him without severe pangs of guilt: his stepfather's public image makes it impossible for Horn to develop a sound sense of self-esteem. For want of a paternal model of self-confidence, self-respect, and self-assertion, Horn is soon to develop an abiding admiration for men of such qualities as supreme authorities, approaching them with a fawning subservience aimed at securing their recognition.[3] By subordinating himself to another's authority, executing his orders, and fulfilling his wishes, Horn hopes to sublimate the desire to cultivate his own intransigent sense of self worth, in effect, seeking compensation for his dimness by serving others' brilliance.

---

[3]See Tilman Moser, "Selbsttherapie einer schweren narzißtischen Störung," *Romane als Krankengeschichten: Über Handke, Meckel und Martin Walser* (Frankfurt/M.: Suhrkamp, 1985) 91-92.

Due to his need for external acknowledgment, which is fulfilled in the course of his speedy professional advancement, Horn worships his boss, Arthur Thiele, as the idol his real father and stepfather could never become. Since Thiele is the first person to entrust Horn with responsibilities, and hence with a sense of usefulness and self-respect, Thiele enjoys the utmost degree of control and authority over Horn. Horn, on his part, treasuring his ostensibly ideal relationship with Thiele, unselfishly sacrifices all his energy and competence, in short, his whole personality for the benefit of the company. Over many years he remains Thiele's right hand, the crown prince of the corporation as it were, his services seeming irreplaceable. After twelve years, however, Horn is confronted with a junior colleague, the young, dynamic, and eminently qualified Dr. Liszt, who, without Horn's knowledge, is hired as his designated successor and rapidly ousts Horn from his privileged position. Horn's professional assignments are suddenly limited to assisting the newcomer. As a consequence, all professional accomplishments are booked on Liszt's record, which invariably injects Horn with a deep assurance of his own incompetence. Liszt's youth and unabashed arrogance deepen Horn's sense of inadequacy. Liszt surpasses Horn in all respects. His unshakable professional, social, and personal self-confidence to the degree of self-glorification are substantiated by his doctoral degree and a wife of aristocratic descent. In the company of the Liszts, Horn, who feels only his abysmal inferiority, is intimidated by their presumptuous affectation.

Naturally Horn's professional demise is instigated by Thiele, whose priorities above all other human values consist of performance, efficiency, and productivity. In his eyes, Horn has fulfilled his part and therefore must be discarded and replaced by a more efficient 'unit.' In the guise of the amicable superior, Thiele shrewdly conceals a scheming and ruthlessly competitive spirit, this being exemplified by an order to Liszt to screen Horn's business letters in order to uncover potential blunders which would justify Horn's debasement. Liszt himself betrays a similar attitude when he writes Horn a letter of recommendation that radically disqualifies his alleged friend. Thus the professional hierarchy is shrouded by the illusion of democracy, the pretense of cordiality and equality between boss and subordinates. Horn, impressionable, benevolent, and slightly naïve, cannot elude these deceptions and remains the loser without a chance. Horn himself intuits only vaguely that he functions merely as a tool, at least he refuses to admit it to himself.

Since his life has become incessant suffering, Horn takes out his frustrations on his wife and children. Upon realizing that his so-called colleagues are responsible for this conduct, however, he separates from his family, which entails the loss of his last remaining human support. Apathetic to and numbed by this harsh reality, Horn, paradoxically, clings to the only relationship left in his life, namely the relationship with his boss and competitor. He shirks all other human intercourse and, in the privacy of his home, overindulges in alcohol. Intoxication, however, only intensifies his compulsive reflections about his personal crisis. Horn has internalized Thiele as an idealized father figure that now rules as a super-ego over all facets of his life to inflict punishment (JL 72). Owing to his injured psychology, all endeavors to repress and escape his mental misery remain futile. Oftentimes Horn's perceptions lack any logic and coherence and thus mirror his state of alienation within a crumbling reality that can no longer be perceived as a cohesive and meaningful whole.

In this reality Thiele embodies the performance principle that keeps Horn under steady pressure.[4] In accordance with Walser's concept of irony, Horn responds to this threat with hysterical self-accusations and self-abasement. Instead of abjuring his boss, he fully accepts Thiele's measures as consequences to his own failure. Horn's weakened self-confidence succeeds in weaving an excruciating inferiority complex throughout his identity, a condition which is manifestly debilitating to his professional persona. Horn blushes, feels ashamed, offers his apologies without reasons, laughs out of insecurity, never defies anyone on principle, all the while judgmentally aware of his ineptitude. Able to blame only himself, he intends to muster all his remaining energies for a successful and vindicating conclusion to a business assignment. He is sent to England to cancel all business relations with one of Thiele's British subsidiaries that fell short of the required profit norms. Convinced that Thiele wants to grant him one final chance to redeem himself, Horn fails to consider the possibility that Thiele may simply seek final proof of his inefficacy. And indeed, on his arrival in England, Horn must realize that he is unable to carry out his tasks. Notwithstanding his optimism that he will return victorious if only he sticks to the habitual, proven strategy of his successful seventeen years, namely to suppress the desire to masturbate, Horn's measures are bound to remain fruitless.[5]

---

[4]See *Jenseits der Liebe*, pp. 7, 36, 86, 93, 114, 122, 125, 163.

[5]This underscores Horn's type as that of the typical underdog, who has been able to survive the stringent performance pressures only by suppressing his genuine needs and primordial drives. He confirms Marcuse's thesis that to ignore one's instincts and to displace gratification are the prerequisites of progress; see *Eros and Civilization*, p. 9. Ewald Dede describes Horn's state as resulting from the repression of libidinal energy; "Der mißverstandene Realismus: Über Martin Walsers Romane *Die Gallistl'sche Krankheit* und *Jenseits der Liebe*," *Literarische Hefte* 52 (1976): 87. Rather one-sided in his Freudian interpretation of the novel is Johan Nedregård's

Upon encountering Keith Heath, Thiele's associate, Horn instinctively recognizes his double. Disfigured by a lingering disease and disillusioned by continued lack of success, Heath can only arouse Horn's sympathies. Heath's separation from his family for professional reasons proves the final pathetic similarity; Horn refrains from terminating the Englishman's contract. Having failed to avail himself of the final opportunity to reingratiate himself with Thiele, Horn gives in to his autoerotic urge and thus squanders the remainder of his vigor, his sole concern being how to explain this failure to his superiors. Again Horn's behavior demonstrates the unbalanced ratio of demanded professional performance and repressed libido as the negative congruence of pleasure principle and reality principle. Hence, the release of libidinal energy negates the adherence to performance norms and becomes a destructive force for Horn. This underscores the degree to which Horn is socially conditioned to adhere to the repressive reality principle and negate his libidinal sphere.

The blocking of natural-instinctual drives accounts for one missing possibility for self-realization. Another presents itself as Horn's longing to end his state of disharmony by achieving union with nature. This natural harmony, the liberation from his work reality, Horn projects into his Keshan rug with its bright "Naturgrund" (JL 30) [nature images], an acquisition for which he had once sacrificed half a year's salary. Horn incurred this expense only shortly after he took employment in Thiele's company and must have unwittingly seen his expectations of life and happiness considerably curtailed. The rug merely represents a material pseudo-substitute for an absent state of harmony which Horn associates with the separation from his family. The fact that he left his rug with his family indicates that his notions of harmony can only be realized through reunification with them. Yet, like the idea of being reunited with his family, Horn's longings for self-realization are desires he consciously and forcibly represses. He has internalized repressive reality to the degree that he mechanically but voluntarily reproduces it himself.

Horn constructs his own mental prison, denying himself a release from his misery. In the moment that he rejects his anguish and feels ready to forswear society forever at the sight of a blooming landscape, he hurls himself abruptly back to reality. As an alternative to his utopian visions of reaching a unity with

---

verdict that *Jenseits der Liebe* is a symbolic portrayal of sexuality; "Der verlorene Zwischenstecker. Über den Assoziationscharakter in Martin Walsers *Jenseits der Liebe* am Beispiel des 2. Kapitels," *Gedenkschrift für Trygve Sagen 1924-1977*, ed. Sverre Dahl, et al., Osloer Beiträge zur Germanistik 3 (Oslo: Oslo UP, 1979) 162. Consequently he neglects Horn's psychological development that leads up to his suicide attempt.

nature — a desire that is voiced more concretely and radically by Gottlieb Zürn in *Jagd* — Horn vaguely considers the positive potential of the Communist Party. But his constant fear of Thiele's accusation that he is a communist (JL 19, 148-50, 153) prevents him from pursuing this political alternative. Contrary to Gallistl, who found personal autonomy by joining a communist group, Horn is rather skeptical in regard to political issues. Eventually, however, the repudiation of communism leads Horn to the crucial realization that his last remaining choice is simply the return to Thiele. Yet, after gaining crucial insights, Horn decides to evade this predicament through his voluntary death.

Franz Horn's psychological development can be viewed in light of Walser's theoretical expositions on irony. Accordingly, *Jenseits der Liebe* demonstrates how the absurd logic of a threatened identity leads to this identity's self-destruction. Horn's alienation is the result of his captivity in a working life that is based on competition. As he had never received an opportunity to develop a genuine sense of self-respect, his only sense of identity stems from his usefulness to Thiele. Thus his personality is determined by socio-economic factors, a fact that Horn accepts (even gratefully) as it allows him to confirm his unstable petty-bourgeois ego under the oppressive external conditions.[6] Thiele's measures of conditioning and domination fill Horn's existence with values which he accepts unquestioningly as his own. In this vein he confirms what Marcuse states as the extreme consequences of alienation, namely

> that the concept of alienation seems to become questionable when the individuals identify themselves with the existence which is imposed on them and have in it their own development and satisfaction. This identification is not illusion but reality. However, the reality constitutes a more progressive state of alienation. The latter has become entirely objective; the subject which is alienated is swallowed up by its alienated existence. This is one dimension, and it is everywhere and in all forms.[7]

It is precisely this one-dimensionality that Horn has absorbed as the only path toward self-realization. Unaware that he was abnegating his genuine individual potential in favor of complying with the demands imposed by the outside world, Horn's way of life turned into a "kleinbürgerliche Unterwerfungs- und

---

[6]See Dieter Liewerscheidt, "Die Anstrengung, ja zu sagen: Martin Walsers Ironie-Konzept und die Romane von 'Jenseits der Liebe' bis 'Brief an Lord Liszt,'" *Literatur für Leser* 9 (1986): 75.

[7]*One-Dimensional Man*, p. 11.

Verzichterklärung" (SI 134) [petty-bourgeois declaration of subordination and resignation] as he internalized Thiele as a surrogate self.

It is not until after his replacement by Liszt that Horn becomes gradually aware of his dominated personality, this awareness being the catalyst for the external plot of *Jenseits der Liebe*. When Thiele blames Horn for his own degradation (JL 20) Horn for the first time denies his allegiance to his boss. At this point he starts cross-examining himself for the real reasons why Thiele has 'dropped him' ("fallengelassen"; JL 20). The first chapter ends with Horn's intent to undertake self-analysis, a resolution that he plans to accomplish by thoroughly reflecting on his relationship with Thiele and Liszt. Thus his trip to England proves to be a journey of self-discovery.[8] As the basis for his self-discovery, however, Horn proclaims his own insignificance. By conceding the outside world total control he practices the petty-bourgeois irony, a process which — if pursued with unflagging consequentiality — leads ultimately to the internal destruction of the individual (SI 40).

Horn's reflections follow this irony in that they condemn themselves to be continually defeated by the outside world. The harder Horn tries to argue against reality, the harsher his arguments turn against himself as he unfailingly reproduces society's repressive dictates by capitulating before Thiele's authority. Horn realizes that he lives vicariously as his existence receives meaning only through Thiele, whose emotions and moods he has substituted for his own. Yet Horn is all but opposed to such an estranged existence. On the contrary, he extols it to the skies, for: "Das war ihm doch viel lieber als das eigene Leben" (JL 46) [He valued that much more than his own life].

Penetrating his negative identity, Horn suddenly feels capable of despising his superiors. His self-confidence being suffocated by his long history of submissiveness, however, he does not possess the strength to break out of his oppressed existence. His efforts to assert genuinely individual thought and his subsequent failures are evidenced in numerous passages, where Horn turns against his superiors only to be immediately refuted by their counter-arguments, advanced by Horn himself as he asserts his negative self — a remarkable assimilation of Thiele. The dialectics of his attempts of self-assertion and his defeats constitute major portions of the novel. It is reminiscent of a boxing bout in which the invincible champion toys with the chanceless underdog. Round after round Horn struggles to get back on his feet only to suffer another knock-down. In the end he acknowledges his defeat and admits his own unworthiness (JL 121-24), taking

---

[8]Waine, *Martin Walser* (Munich: Text + Kritik, 1980) 109.

sides with his superiors by praising their tact, empathy, benevolence, and consideration (JL 119). Once more Horn buttresses whatever restriction external reality has imposed on him, and his negative identity is now definitively determined.

Finally, in a moment of contemptuous self-revelation, Horn cynically unmasks himself as the conformist imbued with hatred and hostility (JL 125). Yet because of his psychological weakness he cannot employ his aggressions for self-defensive purposes. He is now crushed by Thiele's omnipotence and his own decrepitude and debility. Afraid of future abuse through Thiele and Liszt, he plans yet another escape, which, however, for lack of accessible routes, leads him directly back to his employer. Appalled, Horn is again ready to burn all bridges to Thiele as he plans a liberating counter-strike. Yet he still cannot elude the remote control of Thiele's dictates. Hence his aggressions backfire and drive him to suicide. "You had me do your killing" (JL 164), Horn concludes as he executes Thiele's last order. His act of self-liberation is transformed into an act of self-destruction. Once more the absurd logic ("logische Widersinnigkeit") that produces the ironic quality (SI 134) of Horn's thoughts and actions becomes apparent.[9]

When Horn attempts to resolve his desperate quest for self-assertion by suicide, he reaches the point of pure irony ("reine Ironie"; SI 170). Even this reversal, however, is augmented when at last Thiele arrives to save Horn. What drove Horn to self-destruction now paradoxically comes to his rescue. One last time the omnipresence of a power that overrules any alternative to self-determination is confirmed. Social conditions have eradicated all opposition in Horn. This bleak and devastating ending concedes the petty-bourgeois only one kind of freedom: the freedom to invest all his productive energies in the competitive struggle for material profits. The bitter lack of other alternatives formulates a vehement demand for social change, for instead of altruism, solidarity, the sense of community, and friendship there only remains the unrequited longing for these values.

---

[9] See Heike Doane, "Martin Walsers Ironiebegriff: Definition und Spiegelung in drei späten Prosawerken," *Monatshefte* 77 (1985): 209.

4

Writing an End to Misery: *Brief an Lord Liszt*

FOUR YEARS HAVE PASSED in the life of Franz Horn when Walser returns the reader to this character and his sufferings. Like *Jenseits der Liebe*, the sequel illustrates the private misery of an individual which is the consequence of management strategies and production modes, to wit, of socio-economic conditions. In comparison to *Jenseits der Liebe*, the narrated time span in *Brief an Lord Liszt* is even more condensed and covers a period of only approximately sixteen hours, during which Franz Horn writes a letter to his competitor Dr. Horst Liszt. *Brief an Lord Liszt* essentially consists of this letter, using sparsely reported external events merely to establish a spatial and temporal frame. With the exception of these events, which are related through an implied narrator whose vision is more or less identical with that of Horn's own perspective, Walser has his character tell the story in the first person. Hence, *Brief an Lord Liszt* presents itself as a confessional epistolary novel in which Horn attempts to mitigate the distressing facts and events in his life by writing them down.

The crucial insights that Horn gained after his abortive suicide attempt enabled him to liberate himself partially from Thiele's mind control. Although he has distanced himself emotionally from his superior, Thiele still represents a god-like authority for Horn, who has kept his position in the company. Untouchable and invulnerable, the all-too-powerful dictator and egomaniac Thiele rules over the fates of his employees. Since his freedom of action and speech is unconfined, Thiele overtly displays his penchant for cold-blooded, arbitrary action and ruthless moodiness, qualities by which Horn himself had been personally scathed. Claiming his employees' achievements as his own while holding them responsible for any failures, Thiele can insure himself permanent success. Moreover, owing to his undisputed supremacy, he can effortlessly satisfy his insatiable hunger for money, power, and sex. His capitalist leadership has enabled him to bridge the gap between subjective desires and objective reality by attuning his personal demands to society's supply.

Thiele's subordinates, on the other hand, have been conditioned to adopt submissive behavior. Thiele's personality exemplifies the exercise of domination by one individual in order to sustain and enhance its privileged position. Horn seems to have resigned himself to these conditions as he apathetically performs his professional duties. The admission of his inefficiency, albeit only to himself, has put to rest the zeal and ambition of earlier years. Thus Horn has relinquished any desires for self-fulfillment and wallows in a state of unfeeling, lethargic harmony with himself.

Notwithstanding this — admittedly sombre and questionable — equilibrium, Horn is far from reconciled with those who are responsible for his current situation. He is furthermore aware that the impending merger of Thiele's firm with an even larger corporation will exile him to the no man's land of professional anonymity. This realization motivates him to apply for a position with one of Thiele's competitors, Stierle, for it would be only through a change of workplace that Horn could escape his neurotic fixation on his competitor Liszt. Horn's potential new employer, however, foreseeing his own ruin through Thiele's sell-out, destroys his company and kills himself. That which motivates Horn to make a final effort toward personal autonomy simultaneously thwarts this possibility and confirms once again Thiele's status as the almighty capitalist.

Upon learning of Stierle's death, Horn is at once struck by his own insignificance (BL 22), because for four years he has acquiesced in his role as a failure and denied himself a genuine sense of identity — an attitude which Walser describes as "Einübung ins Nichts" (SI 117-52) [rehearsing life without self-identity]. The sudden and acute experience of his own unworthiness compels Horn to confront his identity crisis. The decisive triggering event, however, is a photograph that curiously portrays Liszt in a defenseless pose and thus lets Horn consider the possibility of coming to terms with his own problems while simultaneously getting the better of his antagonist. At this point Horn's nocturnal *tour de force* of self-liberation starts to take its course.

Whereas Horn regarded suicide as his sole alternative in *Jenseits der Liebe*, he seems to have found a more productive solution in *Brief an Lord Liszt*. His attempt to kill himself only proved that he was fully cognizant of the degree to which his existence was controlled by forces beyond his control and, furthermore, that he had accepted the impossibility of achieving personal autonomy. During his business trip to England he gained insights into the laws of production that determine the fate of the individual. Meanwhile the recent developments of Liszt's personal crisis mirror Horn's own, for Liszt too has been ousted from his privileged perch by a new, still younger staff member who now enjoys Thiele's unreserved confidence. Thus, Horn writes from a position of both emotional distance and personal involvement at the same time. He enjoys a cognitive advantage over his competitor, which enables him to illuminate the "historische Dimensionen" (BL 35) ["historical dimensions"; LL 30] of their problem-ridden relationship. Although Horn's preference would be an immediate verbal exchange, he is too intimidated by Liszt's superior self-confidence, his loftiness and repartee, and hence chooses to communicate with him in a monologic fashion. His letter becomes both an act of revenge for and redemption from Liszt's longstanding misjudgments and flawed opinions. Horn will finally pronounce what he has always repressed.[1]

The cynical and surprisingly bold pathos Horn employs from the very beginning of his letter suggests what Horn confirms at the end, namely that the letter will never reach its addressee. Obviously, Horn, who is known to be overly reserved, cautious, and defensive, could only display such pathos in front of himself. Even though he devises his letter as a means to resolve a recent altercation between himself and Liszt, it merely serves him as a pretext to articulate his own dissatisfactions and identity problems.[2] Thus, the process of writing assumes a therapeutic function, with the objective of a psychologically liberating self-analysis.[3] Horn is no longer willing to accept his state of "Machtlosigkeit" (BL 84) ["powerlessness"; LL 79] and wants to refrain from glorifying his own misery and oppression, from practicing the ironic "Lob der Unterdrückung" [praise of suppression] (SI 131) that Walser claims to be so characteristic of the petty-bourgeois. Horn's main incentive is to end his long history of self-denial by mentally overcoming the demands with which he feels confronted and thus gain a new sense of autonomy.[4]

By contrasting their respective careers, Horn intends to prove that in light of recent developments, Liszt's arrogance has lost all grounds for justification, his

---

[1]See Tilman Moser, "Selbsttherapie einer schweren narzißtischen Störung," *Romane als Krankengeschichten: über Handke, Meckel und Martin Walser* (Frankfurt/M.: Suhrkamp, 1985) 101.

[2]Hellmuth Karasek, "Schattenwelt der Angestellten," rev. of *Brief an Lord Liszt*, *Der Spiegel* 18. Oct. 1982: 244.

[3]Heike Doane, "Die Anwesenheit der Macht: Horns Strategie im *Brief an Lord Liszt*," *Martin Walser: International Perspectives*, p. 87; see furthermore Bernd Fischer, "Walser und die Möglichkeiten moderner Erzählliteratur: Beobachtungen zum *Brief an Lord Liszt*," *Martin Walser: International Perspectives*, p. 106.

[4]Doane, "Die Anwesenheit der Macht," p. 93.

strategy being to equate their undesirable situations. Driving this truth home to Liszt requires in the first place Liszt's exposure. By assuming the role of a cross-examiner,[5] Horn is determined to unmask Liszt and to reveal his real motives, an achievement that would weaken his opponent's stance considerably while simultaneously strengthening Horn's own.

Horn's *Brief an Lord Liszt* is an attempt to come to terms with psychological hierarchies among employees, the effects of which well outlast the actual assignment of ranks and power. Horn's desire, however, is to bridge all hierarchical differences between himself and his competitor. He would like to declare himself in solidarity with Liszt, who has himself just experienced a reckoning with which Horn can identify all too vividly. Liszt, after his replacement with Thiele's new superstar Rudolf Ryynänen, separates from his family and apparently becomes an alcoholic (BL 80), although he still refuses to admit his "Sturz" (BL 42) ["fall"; LL 37]. After his rapid professional ascent Liszt had considered himself equal if not superior to his boss and took his executive position for granted. Meanwhile he desperately tries to cling to the last remaining commonalities between himself and Thiele in order to preserve his already battered self-esteem. The fact that Liszt — like Horn before him — is shown the limits of his competence by a yet more competent newcomer proves once more that profit maximization is the underlying principle of capitalism (BL 92). From this Horn infers that between a boss and his subordinates congeniality exists only for the sake of appearance (BL 92). The hierarchy of employees is determined exclusively by the individual's material value to the company, or rather, its director. What Liszt has not yet realized, Horn epitomizes tersely: "Wir sind ihm so viel wert, wie wir für ihn wert sind" (BL 77) ["Our value to him is precisely what we are worth to him"; LL 72-73].

Liszt's conduct demonstrates his refusal to accept his degradation to the same level as Horn, whom he himself had formerly 'dethroned.' Instead he continues to display an air of condescending pretentiousness to preserve his superiority to and his distance from Horn. Horn, on the other hand, admits that he is prepared to bury the competitive hostility between them once and for all. He desires nothing more than for Liszt to accept their situations as equal (BL 86). A confirmed liberal social democrat — he calls himself an "Egalist" (BL 144) ["egalitarian"; LL 140] —, Horn unconditionally identifies with the petty bourgeoisie. If Liszt were to take sides with him, this would forever rid him from his grating inferiority complex. Yet his yearning for Liszt's friendship and

---

[5]Doane, "Die Anwesenheit der Macht," p. 90.

recognition is not reciprocated; instead Liszt insists on his erstwhile authority, which, however, he no longer possesses.

Liszt's claim of superiority gives rise to his excessive self-confidence, which is in turn — as Walser states in an essay — one of the by-products of an aristocratic (*großbürgerlich*) descent. Thus, Liszt's sublime self-esteem ("Erhabenheitsbewußtsein"; SI 104) stigmatizes him as that type of ironic hero whom Walser severely criticizes in the works of Thomas Mann. For Liszt too seems to be endowed with a mental strength that enables him to stand complacently aloof from everything — typifying that casually indifferent "Über-allem-Position" [air of sublimity] (SI 70) for which Walser reprimands the ruling class. By right of birth, Liszt feels entitled to exercise authority and power — "Autorität und Machthabe" (SI 21) in Walser's term's — a capricious notion that allows him to display an air of divine pomposity (BL 144).[6]

To consolidate his own position under the extant social conditions as well as to reinforce these conditions themselves, Liszt claims that his actions follow a purely economic logic that works to the advantage of the system. Since Liszt's personal benefit always coincides miraculously with the benefit of the corporation, he was able to legitimize Horn's debasement as an inevitable consequence of his professional ethics, namely a means to insure the smooth functioning of the system (BL 90). Liszt's remorseless calculations remind Horn of his own ruthlessness of former years, where he himself had worked on the gradual degradation of his predecessor in order to secure his own professional ascent. When Horn had finally become Thiele's right hand, he believed that he had found consummate self-fulfillment in his successful performance within and for the company.[7] What he failed to realize, however, was that he had also become a puppet of Thiele's authority. The reenactment of his evolution through Liszt (and presumably in the foreseeable future through Ryynänen as well) shows the grinding logic of the system's cogs, which enables Thiele to consistently maximize his profits.

In retrospect Horn is aware of his conditioning through the capitalist system. When Thiele declared him a communist for turning 'political,' Horn reconciled himself with the (capitalistic) conditions. Conformism, he now writes, means

---

[6]Horn furthermore adduces evidence of Liszt's narcissism, unscrupulousness, and unassailable self-righteousness (BL 33, 47, 100, 101, 110, 149), qualities that serve Liszt as a means for assurance of self and the humiliation of others. His presumptuousness and self-importance, then, are the result of an overly evolved, god-like self-esteem. Walser quotes Adam Müller, who considers irony a "göttliche Freiheit des Geistes" (SI 81) [divine freedom of the spirit].

[7]See Doane, "Die Anwesenheit der Macht," p. 94.

freedom, at least subjectively speaking (BL 71). Thanks to his successful adjustment, even Horn's instincts have internalized the rules of the system. He notes that his identity is nothing but what others have made of him — he calls himself a "Mimikry-Produkt" (BL 134), a product of socio-economic forces. Yet at the same time, the outside world seems too powerful to suffer harm through one individual's opposition. Hence Horn has been advocating his situation and has joined in with the "Alles-ist-gut-Chor" (BL 98) ["everything-in-the-garden-is-lovely chorus"; LL 93]. His ironic approval of the social circumstances — ironic in the sense of Walser's understanding of irony — not only confirms the efficacy of society's conditioning of the individual, it also initiates in Horn a process of self-recognition.

In accordance with this assertion, Horn will no longer acquiesce to the forces that determine his life. Toward the end of his letter, the thought of surrendering his remaining sense of self activates a new resistance in him that nourishes his desire for personal autonomy.[8] Horn's attitude toward Liszt is still ambivalent; on the one hand he entertains an abysmal aversion against him, on the other he craves Liszt's allegiance, a craving that makes Horn's emotional detachment from his competitor ever so strenuous. Lacking the evidence as to whether Liszt shares his mental misery — Liszt remains inscrutable and unapproachable — Horn eventually decides to break with Liszt for good. He undertakes this withdrawal through writing, and although his abandonment of the antagonist temporarily threatens to revert to self-abdication (BL 138), he feels at last relieved at having severed all ties with Liszt, while having renewed his emotional bonds with his family. Keeping his distance, Horn intends to await the day of Liszt's final fall. Until then he will have to postpone his urge for satisfaction and continue to play his passive part as a cog in the wheel of production. Nevertheless, the acceptance of his dependency and the yielding of all hopes to gain Liszt's allegiance reactivate Horn's quest for self-reliance: "Ich muß selbständig werden" (BL 142) ["I must be independent"; LL 136].

In the final analysis, however, Horn's nocturnal letter simply emerges as another of his characteristic pseudo-solutions. His letter succeeds in emphatically reiterating his condemnation of capitalist ideology, but fails because his message will not reach a recipient. The physical manifestation of his negative experiences aids Horn in overcoming his psychological stress and in rediscovering "die Erträglichkeit des eigenen Lebens" (BL 149) ["the tolerability of one's own life"; LL 144]. Still the durability of these insights is by no means guaranteed, as Horn

---

[8]Doane, "Die Anwesenheit der Macht," p. 97.

also considers such letters to serve as momentary solutions for future conflicts. For the present, his writing has granted him a certain distance from his problems, enabling him to envision a refuge in a relatively unassailable private existence. The warmth and intimacy of the familial circle have to compensate for the impersonal coldness of his working conditions. Although the final scene shows Horn rather elated and with a regenerated sense of perception for his environment, a certain element of irony remains.

Through his conscious efforts to locate the underlying causes of his misery Horn has managed to rid himself of his manic fixation and has gained a partial inner balance on which he can subsist within the given conditions that remain unchanged and ostensibly unchangeable. Horn now looks forward to the imminent merger of his company as it will irrefutably confirm his equality with Liszt. This equality that he so ardently craves, however, will be based on their insignificant roles among an anonymous body of employees. Perhaps Horn has realized that "progressive alienation itself increases the potential of freedom: the more external to the individual the necessary labor becomes, the less does it involve him in the realm of necessity."[9] Thus, Horn continues to fulfill his part as a (however anonymous) functionary in the production process, promoting the "Vernichtung der Schöpfung" (BL 105) ["annihilation of creation"; LL 101). While the efficacy of the modes of production serves the sole purpose of profit maximization, it subverts any potential development toward industrial and political democracy. Hoping to elude this manipulative influence, Horn finds himself seeking solace in the very conditions that had once driven him to suicide. Clearly, his existential glee contains the same amount of ironic affirmation of his working conditions.[10] It appears that Horn consciously devises his professional identity as a role — separate from his private life — to cope with the demands imposed on him. In this vein he would — at least for his private identity — preserve a partially autonomous self.

From Horn's own point of view, his written recapitulation of his alienated identity constitutes a productive response to his perturbed state of mind. As with most of Walser's protagonists, writing becomes a therapeutic means with the purpose of gaining a somewhat objective distance from one's painful experiences (WS 17). Walser sees this therapeutic objective of writing prefigured in Kafka's

---

[9]Marcuse, *Eros and Civilization*, p. 203.

[10]Martin Lüdke, "Wer hat Angst vor Martin Walser?: II. Kein ungeteiltes Vergnügen," *Frankfurter Hefte* 38.1 (1983): 69.

diaries. For Kafka, Walser comments, writing is the final alternative for self-expression (WS 18). Horn himself adopts a tone that shows a close resemblance to that of Kafka, when he writes: "Das Schreiben ersetzt mir jetzt alles. Enggedrängte Buchstaben in einem sonst leeren Zimmer" (BL 134) ["Writing is now my substitute for everything. Cramped handwriting in an otherwise empty room"; LL 130]. Captured in this dead-end street, Horn gives us to understand that his deficiency and the confiscation of his identity by the industrial world are

> der Anlaß und die Bedingung des Schreibens, der Zwang zur Entwicklung des Bewußtseins als einer Waffe gegen diese Not, die sich dann aber als eine Waffe nicht bewährt, sondern nur beweist, daß einer allein wehrlos ist oder hilflos. Aber davon hat er ein Bewußtsein entwickelt. (WS 18)
>
> [the motive and the condition of writing; the compulsion to develop a consciousness as a weapon against this plight, which does not, however, prove itself as a weapon, but merely confirms that one alone is defenseless or helpless. Still, one has become aware of that.]

Accordingly, the only passive resistance against the external conditions that Horn can muster is the consciousness of his defenselessness. In reality, oppression and, consequently, the denial of self-fulfillment continue to exist. By turning colleagues into competitors and by subverting friendship and team spirit, the capitalist economic system functions self-sufficiently. Common interests are confined to materialistic values which undermine ideal ones. The domineering, generally competitive spirit paralyzes the individual's ability to assume a stance of genuine solidarity with others. Horn himself demonstrates his willingness, but is unable to succeed. While the practicability of an oppositional stance against the system would be possible for a collective, it is infinitely more difficult for the individual. Hence, the individual rejects that which could strengthen his position, immobilized by the influence of a system which effectively suppresses the desire for alliance among equals. Eventually it is up to the reader to lend critical attention to this reality.

5

A Clash of Pretenses: *Ein fliehendes Pferd*

WALSER'S FIRST NOVELLA IS preceded by a quotation from Kierkegaard which, more or less overtly, states that the following narrative will contrast or play off two opposite life styles. Thus, Helmut Halm and Klaus Buch, the protagonists, represent two fundamentally different patterns of human behavior and modes of reaction, by means of which both characters strive to achieve a sense of identity in a society governed by appearances and pretense. In such an environment the protagonists unwittingly fall prey to their strategies of survival. Even though the fictional stage is removed from immediate social conflicts, which are suspended by the seemingly idyllic vacational context, Halm's consciousness functions as a sensitive gauge of societal manipulation. Hence the given socio-historical moment determines the protagonists' life strategies.[1]

Halm seems to have recognized that the control society exercises over the individual has ossified into a form of administration in which economic power has been transformed into an anonymous force.[2] Consequently, when society has assumed this form it affects all aspects of human existence and even invalidates the private sector as a bastion for self-realization. Being aware of this bleak reality, Halm's appraisal of society is rather pessimistic, resulting in his emotional and intellectual withdrawal into himself. He declares it his ultimate

---

[1] Reinhard Baumgart writes: "Indem er [Walser] sich auf das scheinbar Allerprivateste einläßt ..., kommt etwas ganz und gar Politisches zum Vorschein: ein soziales System, das keinen Lebenssinn mehr hergibt.... Mit keinem Satz redet die Geschichte zur Lage der Nation. Und doch enthält sie als Ganzes unsere Lage"; "Überlebensspiel mit zwei Opfern," rev. of *Ein fliehendes Pferd*, *Der Spiegel* 27 Feb. 1978: 199. A similar comment is voiced by Herbert Knorr: "Ist hier wirklich Entpolitisierung und Entgeschichtlichung im gang [sic]? Wohl kaum. Denn Walser demonstriert zugleich durch die implizit enthaltene Gesellschaftsanalyse gerade die Bedingtheit der beiden Fluchtwege..."; "Gezähmter Löwe — fliehendes Pferd. Zu Novellen von Goethe und Martin Walser," *Literatur für Leser* 2 (1979): 157. See furthermore Zbigniew Światlowski, "Die Dichtungen Martin Walsers — Selbstbefragung und Literaturexperiment," *Universitas* 35 (1980): 380.

[2] See Marcuse, *Eros and Civilization*, p. 89.

goal to take refuge within his reflections and thus negate all ties with the outside world. In Halm's opinion, society's determination of social values is highly arbitrary and questionable. He therefore forswears a society based on principles of competition and conformism, while his main concern remains to conceal his nonconformist thinking. Because he is acutely insecure and appears almost inept in everyday social intercourse, he ardently wishes to escape reality. His environment, Halm feels, uses knowledge about him in order to condition and subordinate him.[3]

As a tenured secondary school teacher, a prestigious profession in the Federal Republic, Halm has attained relatively high living standards, yet he has paid the price that the system has asked of him: he must realize how the demarcation between his private life and public arena has blurred drastically. The pretense-producing system Halm refers to corresponds to Marcuse's description of a society in which "the productive apparatus tends to become totalitarian to the extent to which it determines not only the socially needed occupations, skills, and attitudes, but also individual needs and aspirations. It thus obliterates the opposition between the private and public existence, between individual and social needs."[4] Still Halm refuses to submit himself to the dogmatic indoctrination that reduces the mind to a product of the societal super-ego and curtails the individual's independence, personal freedom, and critical reason. Nevertheless, the fear that public nonconformism would taint his social prestige motivates him to pretend he is complying with society. After many years of teaching, it is only during his summer vacation that Halm feels safe from the outside world. But even then he prudently keeps up a pseudo-personality and plays the role of the quiet, kind, helpful, and humorous Halm. Although this double identity allows him a small degree of individuality and personal autonomy by hiding his real self behind a façade of conformism,[5] his camouflage is not a wholehearted one. Being highly perceptive, Halm internalizes and intellectualizes his problems. Consequently, his introversion is simply an intellectual solution, which he deems an effective — and, above all, secretive — way to ward off society's impinging norms.

Halm's masquerade is immediately threatened by the appearance of his former school buddy Klaus Buch, for Halm finds himself face to face with his

---

[3] R. Hinton Thomas mentions the "dressierte Natur" of Anselm Kristlein, but neglects the devastating effects social conditioning has on Helmut Halm; "Martin Walser — The Nietzsche Connection," *German Life and Letters* 35 (1981/82): 326.

[4] *One-Dimensional Man*, p. xv.

[5] See Knorr, p. 151.

past, a time before his turning away from society's manipulative dictates. Buch, a show-off and unreflecting conformist, represents an active encroachment of society's demands on Halm's internalized existence.[6] He seems almost like Halm's discarded alter ego returning unexpectedly from the depths of self-oblivion.[7] Since Buch possesses former knowledge of Halm, Halm is again put in a position where he has to meet the expectations and claims of the outside world. This experience is all the more intense because Buch personifies vigor and success, constantly flaunts his virility, his athletic capabilities, and his desire for adventure, in short, his fascination with life (FP 108).

In contrast to Halm, who is 'on the run' from society's performance norms, Buch attempts to surpass them. When he advocates the necessity of physical and sexual fitness, he postulates the unquestionable validity of a pleasure principle. Buch's ostensible self-confidence, vigor, and success confirm Halm's age complex and weaken his already battered sense of identity even more. When Buch illustrates his sex life in vivid terms, he stirs Halm's unpleasant recollection of a previous vacation, where, in front of his own wife, he was shown the limits of his sexual prowess by a veritable love-machine in the adjacent hotel room. Because Halm feels he has suffered a social defeat, he refuses to be competitive and shies away from the society's manipulation of the individual's desires.

These norms are propagated by the mass media, and Halm denounces "FAZ, BILD, Parlament und Schule" (FP 68) ["the national or popular dailies, parliament, and school"; RH 46] for prescribing standards even for leisure activities such as sports and sex, thus degrading those to the status of consumer goods. As Marcuse aptly comments, once social control has reached such an encompassing dimension, societal "domination — in the guise of affluence and liberty — extends to all spheres of private and public existence, integrates all authentic opposition, [and] absorbs all alternatives."[8] This ultimate degree of control society has usurped over the individual, then, motivates the flight of the protagonists. The allegory of the runaway horse depicts visually the escape from

---

[6]Noel L. Thomas, "Martin Walser Rides Again: *Ein fliehendes Pferd*," *Modern Languages* 60 (1979): 169.

[7]In a recent essay, Jonathan P. Clark has interpreted Halm's repression of the past as a mirror of a national problematic. Halm is seen as representative of a Germany that, under the burden of the past, finds itself in an identity crisis. Clark's arguments are compelling and do not interfere with this author's reading; see "A Subjective Confrontation with the German Past in *Ein fliehendes Pferd*," *Martin Walser: International Perspectives*, pp. 47-58.

[8]*One-Dimensional Man*, p. 38.

public demands, an escape to a short-lived and untenable freedom from society's dictates, which, in the guise of Klaus Buch who recaptures and subdues the farmer's runaway horse, are catching up rapidly to reinstate their full control.[9]

Knowing full well from past experiences that he could not achieve the publicly demanded performance anyway, Halm anxiously avoids any sexual contact with his wife.[10] When he admits to himself, however, "Wollen, ja. Tun, nein" (FP 68) ["To desire it, yes. To do it, no"; RH 45], he not only rejects society's dictates but also suppresses his own individual desires when they coincide (although to a lesser degree) with these demands. Through the conscious denial of such genuine longings, Halm preserves his freedom of will — although in a negative sense. On the other hand such self-discipline carries the very concept of individuality to an absurd level.[11] Consequently, Halm's internalizing strategies disallow productive counteraction from the outset; on the contrary, they actually serve to maintain the *status quo*, confining him to a state of utter passivity.

Buch, by contrast, supersedes society's dictates and bolsters his ego through his role as an over-achiever. In Halm's opinion Buch even uses his much younger wife as a trophy (FP 21) to strengthen his own self-confidence. While Buch seeks continual proof of his wife's affection, he at the same time forbids her to be artistically active and subjugates her to demands that she is unable to meet. What Halm does not realize, however, is that Buch's appearance is likewise a socially conditioned camouflage. Professional instability and lack of success overshadow Buch's life, which in reality is ruled by frustration, fear, and despair. Buch's social insecurity — although he invests all his energy in his journalistic work he remains rather unsuccessful — limits his financial possibilities on which the fulfillment of materialistic leisure norms in a capitalist system depends to a large extent. By compulsively meeting the demands of society and surpassing them, Buch compensates for the limitations of his individual sphere of activity. Sex for him has become the paramount sector for self-actualization, since it remains the only facet of his life where he can be assured that his efforts will be acknowl-

---

[9]The only critic to suggest the horse as a symbol of freedom has been Hans Erich Struck, *Martin Walser: Ein fliehendes Pferd*, Oldenbourg Interpretationen 27 (Munich: Oldenbourg, 1988) 30.

[10]He even faintly considers the idea of raping or murdering Sabine (FP 66, 103) in order to elude the possibility of her reproaching him with sexual impotence.

[11]Walser's concept of the petty-bourgeois ironic hero here applies to Halm. Since he has no chance of fulfilling his wishes he turns them into something undesirable so he can take pride in willfully denying them.

edged. Yet, his hedonistic egocentrism has isolated and alienated him from others of whom he can only think as competitors.

In view of Buch's financial situation, his ultimate notion of happiness — the everlasting escape to paradise, namely the Bahamas — is simply utopian cliché of leisure that he seems to have borrowed from the public opinion sector. Lacking Halm's intellectual capacity, Buch's persistent endeavors to affirm his own identity by assimilating the prevailing ideology appear desperate. His compulsive identification with the system prevents him from discovering that he is actually controlled by public opinion. By blaming himself for his professional failure, he promotes the consolidation of society's new forms of control which Marcuse describes as follows: "No matter how much such needs [that society prescribes] may have become the individual's own, reproduced and fortified by the conditions of his existence; no matter how much he identifies himself with them and finds himself in their satisfaction, they continue to be what they were from the beginning — products of a society whose dominant interest demands repression."[12]

It may appear that the opposing escape strategies of the two antagonists, marked by Halm's secretive introversion and Buch's exaggerated extroversion, are determined by their differently conditioned attitudes toward sexuality. From a broader perspective, however, they result directly from the characters' biographies. As in Walser's other novels, the protagonist's biographical background can be established from a multitude of scattered fragments. Thus, Halm stems from a petty-bourgeois context — his father had been employed as a waiter — and still admits to himself his affiliation to this social class, while on the exterior he produces the bourgeois attitude and principles of the public school teacher. Halm remembers Buch to be the offspring of a wealthy grand-bourgeois family whose lavish mansion he only dared admire from the distance. Hence Halm never was able to completely overcome his inferiority complex with regard to persons who were socially superior, a complex that he has long internalized.

Halm is very much aware of class distinctions, social injustice, and, specifically, the pseudo-value of certain social norms. He now enthusiastically renounces the consumer society in which he himself is firmly entrenched, but he cannot help avert the temptation of the outside world that instills in him a desperate craving for sexual encounters (FP 9). In the course of events, Helene

---

[12]*One-Dimensional Man*, p. 5.

Buch personifies the sexual charms which Halm finds so alluring.[13] Clearly, Halm is attracted by the outside world and is by no means content in his internal hiding place. For this reason he envisions a state of self-isolation that would render him completely untouchable, while at the same time he insists on his wife's unflagging support of his life style.

At forty-six Halm refuses to compete with the still so youthful former friend, who never ceases to flaunt his sexual superiority. By encouraging Halm to engage in sexual activity, Buch, during the final sailing episode, drives Halm even deeper into his introversion. At last, provoked by Buch's verbal affront, and justifiably frightened by his potentially lethal sailing tactics, Halm can no longer keep up his assumed outward identity and causes the accident. Halm's only spontaneous act results in the fall of his antagonist. Halm himself, however, momentarily stripped of his "Urlaubsrolle" (FP 15) ["vacation role"; RH 5] and recognized by Buch's last glance, also suffers the decisive defeat in his escape attempts. In this life-threatening situation he must experience the limits of his strategies of self-realization through internalization.

When Halm finally gains insight into the pseudo-existence of the hated but envied Buch, he understands that neither his 'inner emigration' nor Buch's escape into the socially imposed performance standards foster a working symbiosis of the individual and society. After he has unmasked both his and Buch's way of life as conscious self-deception, his ego ventures out of its submersion and he confesses to Sabine. Halm's state of disillusionment coincides with a level of consciousness that enables him to evaluate and communicate past events. Desisting from his previous concerns about his secret self, his communicative urge, which expressed itself earlier in his letter to Klaus Buch,[14] now gains the upper hand. Although this letter never reached its addressee, Halm had felt a wave of relief at his written self-confession. Whereas he could not draw any conclusions then, he now undertakes his confession in the third person. This shows a degree of objectivity which Halm has attained toward himself and which might enable him to confront his problems.[15] His openness with his wife suggests a first timid step toward social bonds. The prospects of a new life that had appalled him earlier in a dream he now envisions to realize in communion with Sabine.

---

[13]See *Ein fliehendes Pferd*, pp. 47, 49, 79, 95, 98.

[14]Donald Haase, "Martin Walser's *Ein fliehendes Pferd* and the Tradition of Repetitive Confession," *32nd Mountain Interstate Foreign Language Conference*, ed. Gregorio C. Martín (Winston Salem, N.C., 1984) 140, 141.

[15]Anthony Waine, *Martin Walser* (Munich: Text + Kritik, 1980) 119.

Since the modification of Halm's escape strategies might produce a constructive life plan, Halm and Buch should not be considered similar losers.[16] Moreover, it is debatable whether the open ending must be interpreted as a dead-end street for the characters, leaving no alternatives for either one.[17] One might claim that they have learned from each other's weaknesses, which, of course, cannot be proved with regard to Buch. At least Halm, through his narration, envisages a communicative solution. He utterly accepts Sabine's remonstrance that she may not believe everything that he is going to tell her, which for him would constitute the real solution (FP 151). Through Sabine's intervention his narration would develop into a self-revealing dialogue. And only if his confession turned into a conversation would Halm's self-therapeutic efforts be rewarded.

When Halm finally starts to tell Sabine his "Abenteuer" (FP 28) ["adventure"; RH 15], he reawakens his repressed past and transforms it again into "Erzählbare[s]" (FP 28) [a tellable story]. It is the ability to accept the past as an essential constituent of a continually broadening perspective on life, which should release Halm from his emotional blockade.[18] The ending indicates a new sense of self, which for Halm is attainable only within the most intimate, private context. The insights he has gained into the deforming social mechanisms can prevent their impingement on the private sector, if he is willing to discuss these insights with a communicative partner. Only when the private sphere remains untainted by society's dictates can it stand as a bastion against the outside world. As the social conditions that the text discloses are disquietingly static and stifling, they can only be changed by confronting, questioning, and provoking them. The system's alleged objective nature that penetrates the individual's most subjective sphere demands critical examination. This is what Walser's novella asks of the reader.

---

[16]Marcel Reich-Ranicki, "Martin Walser," *Entgegnung. Zur deutschen Literatur der siebziger Jahre*, (Stuttgart: Deutsche Verlags-Anstalt, 1979) 172.

[17]Heike Doane, "Innen- und Außenwelt in Martin Walser's [sic] Novelle *Ein fliehendes Pferd*," *German Studies Review* 3 (1980): 83.

[18]Waltraud Wiethölter, by contrast, suggests the impossibility of change by proclaiming the infinite self-referentiality of the text; "'Otto' — oder sind Goethes *Wahlverwandtschaften* auf den Hund gekommen? Anmerkungen zu Martin Walsers Novelle *Ein fliehendes Pferd*," *Zeitschrift für deutsche Philologie* 102 (1983): 258.

6

Sexuality and Death; or, The Dialectics of Domination: *Brandung*

IN *BRANDUNG* HELMUT HALM, now fifty-five years of age, accepts a position as visiting lecturer at Washington University in Oakland, California (a fictionalized version of Berkeley). In the novel, Halm confirms that he and his wife overcame that obnoxiously show-offish Klaus Buch with a gain of unity (B 123). However, the invitation to teach from Halm's old friend Rainer Mersjohann, now chairman of the German Department at Washington University, clouds this state of private harmony, for Halm is suddenly obsessed with the desire to escape from "dieser verwirkten deutschen Gegend" (B 27) ["this disillusioning German environment"; Br 21]. In accordance with Halm's pervasive sentiment in *Ein fliehendes Pferd*, that everything is possible so long as others have no knowledge of him (FP 13), the hope for a new beginning is reason enough for his feverish optimism. Just as Halm habitually escapes from his working life to his lakeside vacation in *Ein fliehendes Pferd*, his next escape attempt leads him to California, where he again collides with Buchian views as represented by the state of California and its way of life. Once more the setting in *Brandung* is removed from immediate social conflicts, and the transience of Halm's stay invokes the impression of an exotic vacation experience.[1] Accordingly, the plot centers upon the main character's personal problems. Following the succinct compactness of *Ein fliehendes Pferd*, Walser, appropriate to the scope and intensity of the conflict, presents an expansive web of events.

Thus *Brandung* continues to develop the conflicting life styles of Halm and Buch. Buch's superficial existence of unquestioning conformism under capitalist conditions, however, is now projected onto the splendor of Halm's new surroundings. This intensified 'counter-sphere' in *Brandung* appears so tempting

---

[1]See Mark E. Cory, "Romancing America: Reflections of Pocahontas in Contemporary German Fiction," *German Quarterly* 62 (1989): 325. Cory examines novels by several authors (including Walser), who grant their male protagonists a temporary "escape, either from a painful personal past or from the constricting conventions of a proper European academic existence or both."

that Halm is suddenly provoked to change into some kind of Klaus Buch.[2] His unceasing self-reflections, however, prevent him from escaping his introversion. He cannot overcome his fear of sexual vulnerability, which again results from the encroachment of society's demands for greater sexual freedom onto the preferences and inclinations of the individual. Like *Ein fliehendes Pferd*, *Brandung* illustrates Halm's sexual problems, although to understand their social origins a reading of the novella seems necessary.

The temporary change of scenery offers Halm the opportunity of escaping the vestiges of his everyday German existence, particularly those imposed by his professional milieu. Comparable to Franz Horn's position within a corporate hierarchy, Halm has to cope with his superiors. As a tenured member of the teaching staff in a state-run school, Halm, however, does not find himself professionally dependent on others. Nevertheless — and this again is attributable to his unstable self-confidence as a petty-bourgeois descendent — he has developed both an inferiority complex toward and a psychological fixation on one of his superiors, whom, evidently for his upper class background, Halm both envies and admires. Parallel to the events in *Brief an Lord Liszt*, where Horn is gradually replaced by a newcomer, this younger colleague has passed Horn in the staff hierarchy. Although in California Halm is thrilled by the idea of leaving behind all these concerns, he cannot liberate himself from being mentally dominated by his presumable opponent, who, like a 'Big Brother' looms over him with his ubiquitous presence. Moreover it is now Rainer Mersjohann who exercises the domineering influence of a superior and by whose presence (actual or imagined) Halm feels perpetually censored.

At first, however, the radiant, blossoming land with its glorious weather, its glistening bay, its nocturnal cicada choruses, and sun-tanned, youthful crowds convinces Halm that life is worth living (B 271). Above all, it is the temptation of attractive females through which the outside world entices him. Although convinced of his immunity to any kind of sexual provocation since his last encounter with Klaus and Helene Buch, the dazzled Halm falls prey to the charms of the new environment. Despite his hopes in *Ein fliehendes Pferd* that the torture of sexual activity would soon be over (FP 67), he involuntarily but consciously becomes a victim of the new splendor of life surrounding him. His perception of the outside world is a direct reflection of his repressed sexuality — everywhere

---

[2]See Heinz D. Osterle, "Wo viel Schatten ist, ist auch viel Licht. Eindrücke eines verhinderten Einwanderers," Interview with Martin Walser, *Bilder von Amerika: Gespräche mit deutschen Schriftstellern*, ed. Heinz D. Osterle (Münster: Englisch Amerikanische Studien, 1987) 225.

he looks life shows erotic attributes (B 22, 45, 67, 211, 235), haunting him even in his dreams (B 276-77). Yet these are merely secondary symptoms. The center of Halm's attention belongs to the twenty-two-year-old undergraduate Fran Webb in his conversation class, who causes in him an emotional turmoil of major proportions.

Halm is stricken in part by the sudden awareness of his own age, but more significantly by the remorse of missed opportunities for the pleasures of life. Entrapped by an age complex and a general existential pessimism of almost critical dimensions, Halm wishes nothing more than to venture back into the maelstrom of life. Hence he offers no resistance when Fran Webb reactivates his repressed sexual needs and lures him out of his self-seclusion back to the 'pleasure front.' Fascinated with her radiancy, he forces himself to adjust to the ideals of her life; determined to reverse the aging process, he swears to reduce his consumption of alcohol and cigars to a minimum (B 217). Halm feels so inspired by the brilliance of his new environment that he decides to conform fully to society's demands for greater physical and thus sexual capability, while realizing that he does so in a Buchian manner (B 195).

Halm suddenly advocates the compulsive enjoyment of life and obeys society's dictates to conform even in the private sector. He accepts the societally postulated validity of leisure norms, ignoring the fact that these standards originate in a capitalist ideology predominantly rooted in social prestige and material affluence. Halm thus succumbs to ideals that are propagated by the mass media and that create the illusion of freedom and equality while effacing actual social hierarchies. The illusion of freedom virtually eliminates the individual's willingness and ability to reflect on the anonymous societal apparatus since the inequalities, oppression, and exploitation that exist in reality (although not specifically addressed within the social context of *Brandung*) are veiled, that is, are made bearable. Like Franz Horn, who in *Brief an Lord Liszt* joins in with the conformist "Alles-ist-gut-Chor" (BL 98) ["everything-in-the-garden-is-lovely chorus"; LL 93], Halm tends to unquestioningly accept the given conditions and considers them an irreversible "So-ist-es-schlechthin" (B 239) ["That's the way it is"; Br 228]. In this manner he reaffirms Franz Horn's motto of the liberating effects of conformism, "Wer mitmacht, kommt sich frei vor" (BL 71) ["Those who conform think of themselves as free"; LL 66].

Owing to the overwhelming impact of the temptations that stir in him a riot of long repressed emotions, Halm at first considers the possibility of confiding in his wife; the newly inflamed wish to take on the temptation, however, proves stronger. Shortly after that Halm can no longer rely on Sabine's moral support, since she has to return to her dying father. Now each encounter with Fran torments Halm even more, to the extent that he threatens to lose his composure (B 184). Unable to find an outlet for his surplus sexual energy, Halm's inner commotion is further complicated by the desire to conceal and justify to himself this socially unseemly teacher-student affair that, of course, never transcends the realm of his imagination. Unable to come to terms with his double identity within society, he envisages relief by verbalizing his problems, that is, by fictionalizing them and imparting them to a potential listener (B 125). Thus, he could still maintain his anonymity while giving vent to his communicative needs. Forced to bear the situation alone, however, Halm is obsessed with the fear of making a fool of himself. His guilty conscience in combination with his general insecurity lead him to an image of himself as a comical-grotesque figure who never misses an opportunity to expose his foibles.

Whereas the students act "selbstvergessen" (B 45) ["obliviously"; Br 38], the opposite is the case with Halm. He is incapable of meeting anybody's eye (B 56, 57), lapses into stuttering (B 62, 70), or is at a loss for words (B 69). He himself perceives his actions and reactions as unnatural, contrived, and most ludicrous. As in *Ein fliehendes Pferd*, society's manipulative influence as the ultimate organ of censorship becomes transparent. The fact that he has internalized society's demands, Halm admits, is his chief weakness (B 186); and yet he cannot remedy his plight. Ironically, he, the author of a manuscript on Nietzsche, fancies himself surrounded by more powerful entities, in front of whom he, the eternally inferior one, must constantly justify his presence.[3] Halm's contacts with Carol Elrod, the departmental secretary, underscore his delusion of inferiority. By virtue of her wit and repartee she is in firm control of the administrative affairs of the German department and becomes a control figure of sorts for Halm. Since she sees through him from the very beginning and taunts him about his secret infatuation with Fran Webb, Halm feels pressured to exonerate himself through desperate attempts at self-justification and confession. He is continually driven back to Carol, and although she never fails to penetrate his sociable façade (e.g. B 121), he longs for her negative feedback and considers her his only confidante (B 194).

His relationship with Rainer Mersjohann is similar. In spite of his fear of and respect for the chairman, Halm feels a peculiar attraction to him. His interaction with Mersjohann reinforces the weakness Halm exhibits in every facet of his

---

[3]See Manfred Dutschke, "Jenseits der Wellen könnte man schwimmen — einige Bemerkungen zu Martin Walsers 'Brandung,'" *German Studies in India* 10 (1986): 4; furthermore Hellmuth Karasek, "Malvolio in Kalifornien," rev. of *Brandung, Der Spiegel* 26 Aug. 1985: 159.

social life. Every contact with the outside world conveys a threat to him, and thus he struggles not to lose face, even as he suffers considerable defeats. Consequently, his main objective is not to attract attention, assuming a role as in the novella, solely for the purpose of concealing his true self. Halm's interpersonal inadequacies belie his conviction that he has attained a lasting untouchability; social intercourse becomes increasingly problematical, requiring the concentration of all his powers of deception to remain incognito. He is meanwhile riddled with doubt, subjecting each word and action to merciless scrutiny. Only in solitude do his anxieties dissipate temporarily.

Still this emotional clearing cannot insulate Halm from recognizing the absurdity of his attempts against introversion. The division of his ego into "Ich-Halm" ["I-Halm"] and "Er-Halm" ["He-Halm"] (e.g. B 60, 68; Br 53, 61) illustrates his split identity: the former, the rational, arguing man of reason, the latter, the irrational self of emotion; the reproachfully attacking I versus the defensively acting He. This inner conflict governs Halm's relationship with Fran Webb, which is in essence mediated through his choice of literature. These literary works serve both as a medium for Halm's indirect articulation of his secret emotions and as a mirror of his wavering attitude toward his purely platonic relationship with Fran Webb.[4] The reading of Faulkner's narrative *The Hamlet* finally induces Er-Halm to identify with the main character Labove, who tries to rape one of his female students in the classroom (B 245). Halm had previously considered such violent measures, even entertaining murderous fantasies (B 236, 249). His unrequited infatuation combined with his inhibitions provoke in him a perverse lust to kill or, conversely, elicit suicidal fantasies (B 236, 272-73).

The vacillation between homicide and suicide is analogous to Halm's conflict between internal and external existence. On the one hand, Halm would like to emerge from his introversion, but his awareness of the outside world of pretenses continually deters him. The result is a state of abeyance due to insecurity. Thus, Halm drifts between the two modes of existence of Halm and Buch, or differently put: between intellect and instincts, the yearning for death and the urge to live,[5] or, between an intellectual isolation *à la* Nietzsche and consumerism. The main

---

[4]Siegfried Mews, "Martin Walsers *Brandung*: Ein deutscher Campus-Roman?," *German Quarterly* 60 (1987): 225.

[5]Heinrich Vormweg, "Bittersüß die Schmerzen des Alterns," rev. of *Brandung*, *Süddeutsche Zeitung* 31 Aug. 1985: 104.

issue, however, is sexuality in general, exemplified through the recurring image of the "Brandung" that is freighted with unmistakably sexual attributes (B 94, 225). In Halm's view, Fran Webb embodies the feminine and erotic principle (B 212, 236) and personifies the center of the challenges of life. At the same time she becomes — like Klaus Buch — the representative *par excellence* of society's leisure norms, enticing and manipulating Halm with her feminine charms and feigned innocence.

As Fran Webb assumes the authority of a dominating mistress on whom Halm is dependent, the master-servant theme of *Seelenarbeit* manifests itself in *Brandung* on an erotic plane.[6] Perceiving his relationship with Fran as that of a dog to a master, Halm laments his dependency (B 262). Yet the intensity of his rekindled, though unfulfilled sexual needs deeply disturbs his already shaky inner balance, causing him to experience an acute sense of estrangement from life. In part he is now inclined to yield to his urge for sexual "Hemmungslosigkeit" (B 186) ["recklessness"; Br 177] and seek unrestricted fulfillment of his undeniable sexual desires. Clinging to the role of the intellectual, however, Halm persistently seeks theoretical proof that sexual activity lacks all justification outside of the purpose of procreation (B 270). He wants to be convinced that sex is nothing but a highly repugnant, mechanic "Pseudodienst" (B 164) ["pseudoservice"; Br 155] that one performs simply to experience physical pleasure.

By questioning the validity of sexual activity, Halm — in Marcuse's words — tries to muster "the full force of civilized morality against the use of the body as mere object, means, instrument of pleasure."[7] His strategy is clearly to establish a rational construct that will successfully invalidate the existence of his sexual desires and thus defuse the Californian temptation. Yet Halm also questions the substance of intellectual knowledge and finally becomes disillusioned with an existence that seems to lack both intellectual and instinctual justification. While in *Ein fliehendes Pferd* Halm was at pains to ward off any sexual advances from his wife, he nevertheless felt a strong desire to indulge. In *Brandung* Halm gives in to his desires — now it is he who seduces Sabine (B 152, 165). Far from finding satisfaction in sexual intercourse with her, Halm desperately tries to refute his sexual desires altogether. Just like Xaver Zürn in *Seelenarbeit*, who thinks that he is not alive for want of sexual experiences, Halm is continuously plagued by the same sense of discontent, of incompleteness and

---

[6]See Martin Halter, "Der alte Mann und das Mädchen," rev. of *Brandung*, *Badische Zeitung* 11 Sept. 1985: 8.

[7]*Eros and Civilization*, p. 183.

lack. Hence, during sexual intercourse with his wife his innermost desire is to disappear in her entirely and forever and thus regress to a gender-combining existence of an androgynous whole.

Due to the invariably utopian character of his back-to-the-womb fantasies, Halm continues to mentally succumb to Fran Webb's attraction. The frustration of being confined to verbal orgasms during their literary conversations almost drives him to the extremes of murder and rape. Thus, her effect on Halm is ambiguous: while "Ich-Halm" reacts with aversion and antipathy, "Er-Halm" is overwhelmed. Yet, Halm tries to discredit his fascination as "Brandungslärm" (B 68) ["Noise of the surf"; Br 61], as the purely physical temptations of external life. However, his symbolic attempt to overcome these temptations by swimming beyond the breakers fails (B 91); he lacks determination when faced with the ocean's overwhelming turbulence and his efforts result merely in aching joints. Moreover, the ironic portrayal of this incident exposes Halm's failure, detached from his past, to reaffirm his ego through a heroic venture.

Back in Germany, the influence of California is finally eradicated, and Halm recognizes that his inner commotion was merely "much ado about nothing" (B 308). However, in a melodramatic turn of events, he is informed about Fran's fatal accident in a landslide. The fact that he can scarcely satiate his interest in the newspaper clipping reveals that Halm's genuine reaction is great relief. Confirming in retrospect Fran's earlier statement, "Studies of rapists have shown that the destruction of what was desired stops the desire" (B 249), her death frees him from her domination. Halm even revels in postulating his own contribution to Fran's death, for the crutches she had had to use through his fault — he had caused an accident when he danced with her while heavily intoxicated — could have prevented her from getting out of her car (B 311). His earlier thoughts of murdering her explain the note of self-contentment in his reaction. In both *Ein fliehendes Pferd* and *Brandung* Halm's escape strategies ultimately lead to accidents. Undoubtedly, they are the manifestation of Halm's suicidal aggressions externalized, his wish to destroy the external, manipulative pretenses that he perceives as both temptation and threat.

Finally it is a dream which initiates in Halm a new sense of inner balance. After four months of successfully adhering to his ironic motto that one should do "was man nicht will" (B 238) ["what one doesn't want"; Br 227], Halm finally realizes that the unrelenting struggle against one's own desires leads "zu NICHTS als zur Erschöpfung" (SI 148) [to nothing but exhaustion], and his forced affirmative pose toward the given conditions yields to a new understanding of self. No longer suppressing his desire to confess and no longer convinced of having to fight his battle furtively, Halm once again rediscovers the comforting presence of his wife. His final confession to her will be a retelling of the novel. Thus, like in *Ein fliehendes Pferd*, the beginning of Halm's narration marks the end of an inner struggle, that is, a completed mental process that has reached the level of communicability. When Halm confides in his wife, he achieves precisely that solution he had earlier envisioned: a gain in unity and intimacy.

As in the novella, the story begins anew with the narration of Helmut Halm, who rises from a figural medium to an authorial narrator. The story retold by Halm in the third person thus assumes the quality of fiction. In this sense Halm acts like the author himself, that is, in a therapeutic manner, by verbalizing the lack of identity that compels Walser to write and Halm to narrate.[8] The confessional narration as a self-therapy of sorts can be linked in essence to the author's concept of writing. Halm's final confessions, then, are analogous to the author's literary-creative act of self-analysis and reflection. Still, Walser insists that the experience of a personal lack must always be considered a consequence of social influences.[9] The fictitious character constantly struggles to come to terms with internal as well as external deficiencies and reflects on the source of his suffering. By penetrating the subjective perspective of the character and examining the character's limited options of self-actualization, the reader is left to draw his own conclusions about a society in which humans are perceived to communicate like battleships (FP 37). For Walser, "Leiden und Handeln" [affliction and action] constitute a dialectical movement the synthesis of which is achieved in the act of writing.[10] In *Ein fliehendes Pferd* and *Brandung* this concept is projected onto the main character Helmut Halm, who counteracts his conscious self-deception (affliction) through productive self-therapeutic measures (action). His timid, though honest, recourse to his wife, to communication in general, subtly counters the conditioning forces of the outside world.

---

[8]Martin Walser, "Wer ist ein Schriftsteller," p. 37. Volker Bohn has also put Halm's retelling in analogy to Walser's writing; cf. "Ein genau geschlagener Zirkel: Über 'Ein fliehendes Pferd,'" *Martin Walser*, ed. Klaus Siblewski (Frankfurt/M.: Suhrkamp, 1981) 167, note 16.

[9]Martin Walser, "Ein Blick durchs umgekehrte Fernrohr," *Gesellschaftspolitische Aspekte in Martin Walsers Kristlein-Trilogie*, by Heike Doane (Bonn: Bouvier, 1978) 1.

[10]Martin Walser, "Wer ist ein Schriftsteller," p. 41.

The Dark Side of Sunny California: Excursus on *Meßmers Gedanken*

MEßMERS GEDANKEN CAPTURE the frustrations and depressions smoldering beneath the surface of *Brandung*, taking up the thread of frequent, veiled references to a certain Meßmer, Halm's predecessor at Washington University. Halm persistently ignored his secretary's admonitions to read the diary-like "Geschichte des unglücklichen Bewußtseins" (MG 48) [history of an unhappy consciousness], preferring instead to submerge himself in the unchallenging adventurousness of Kirk Elrod's *Inspiration Inn*, a novel that more readily lives up to his reawakened urge to live ("Lebensbedürfnis"; B 186) in his new environment, California. For this reason, *Meßmers Gedanken* were not integrated in *Brandung*, in accordance with Walser's original plan, but ended up as a separate publication.

The aphorisms reveal the depth of an existential crisis in which Meßmer struggles against the almost completed disintegration of his identity. Meßmer perceives the outside world as a threatening front of "Gewalt, Macht, Übermacht" (MG 21) [force, power, omnipotence] that undermines the most personal facets of his life, to the extent of equating all human contacts with plain hostility. Although he claims that the deformations of his identity are traceable to the effects of capitalism (MG 19), Meßmer admits that, except for this global condemnation of the system, his statements contain "[n]ichts Politisches" (MG 94) [nothing political]. While in Walser's novels the oppressive forces are typically personified in the company directors, competitors, or other antagonists, in *Meßmers Gedanken* these hostile entities have become faceless — Meßmer speaks merely of 'others' ("anderen"), whose positions he has assimilated: "Aus mir spreche nicht ich, sondern der Widerspruch" (MG 41) [It is not I, but the contradiction that speaks through me].

Utterly defenseless against the crushing might of the outside world, Meßmer experiences his life as a form of non-existence — "Ich lebe wie nicht" (MG 75) [I live as if I didn't]. His identity, or rather, his non-identity, consists of a plethora of roles that have become his second nature.[1] The expression of his

---

[1] See *Meßmers Gedanken*, pp. 7, 36-28, 33, 42, 52.

thoughts in the first, second, and third person (while many a first-person utterance ends with the *inquit* formula "denkt Meßmer") attests to Meßmer's insight into his self-alienation. Hence he describes himself as being composed of incompatible and contradictory fragments that cannot be joined together to shape a whole (MG 48). Instead of a unique entity, Meßmer's personality represents a highly adaptable, conforming non-character: "Allgemeiner als ich, kann [sic] man nicht sein" (MG 17) [It is impossible to be more indistinct than myself]. Meßmer's self-denial resounds with pain and resignation: "Ich möchte entlassen werden von mir" (MG 75) [I would like to be released from myself]. He therefore feels more alive among the dead and often meditates on dying or being dead[2] as he cannot find closeness to another human (MG 47).

Meßmer's self-imposed isolation is so successful that, unable to invest any personal significance in external events, he becomes trapped in his own opaque consciousness. His fragmented self has relinquished all hope, resistance, and fear in acceptance of the irreversible dissolution of his identity. Thus Meßmer embodies the apogee of alienation in Walser's prose works. Moreover his mental stream is carried by a self-destructive ironic counter-logic. Meßmer has introjected the automatic affirmation of the given external circumstances and has erased all residues of individual thought.

> Immer wenn ich Nein sagen will, sage ich Ja. Das ist vorwegtrainiert, eingeübt. *Nein* wird schon im Vorfeld der Sprache *Ja*. Es bedarf dazu keiner Mitwirkung meinerseits. (MG 28)
>
> [Whenever I want to say No I say Yes. That is preconditioned, rehearsed. *No* turns to *Yes* already in the prelingual sphere. No effort is required on my part.]

What remains most striking, however, is the paradoxical fact that it is Meßmer himself whose tortured confessions of non-identity give testimony to his desolate quandary. Franz Horn, who in *Jenseits der Liebe* reaches the very same dead-end, resorts to suicide. Meßmer, on the other hand, continues to live his pseudo-existence, trying to suffocate his desolation under an impervious layer of cynicism that, however therapeutic, exposes his very insignificance: "Wenn ich meine Mütze aufsetze, bin ich, denkt Meßmer" (MG 106) [When I put on my hat, I am, Meßmer thinks]. While this thought echoes Descartes' existential conclusion *cogito, ergo sum*, Meßmer's intentions of self-assertion express the desire to be

---

[2] See especially pp. 59-63, 89, 91, 102, 103.

a nobody, a non-entity. Meßmer's resolute determination to withdraw from life itself, his apathy and self-abdication, appear like an opposite alternative to Helmut Halm's efforts to participate in the pleasures of life. Yet Meßmer never comes to life as a fleshed-out character, he remains merely a voice of fragmentary impressions, a self-conscious non-identity. Hence he is an example of a potentially livable, albeit deterring for self-destructive, and thus untenable form of existence.

7

Oppression by Self-Discipline: *Seelenarbeit*

IN THE NOVEL *SEELENARBEIT*, Walser chooses a master-servant relationship to depict the classical form of domination portrayed in two earlier plays: the relationship between the capitalist Krott and the servant/waiter Ludwig in *Überlebensgroß Herr Krott* (1964; Mr. Krott, Larger Than Life) and — similar to *Seelenarbeit* — the conflicting perspectives of the director and his chauffeur in *Der Abstecher* (1961; *The Detour*, 1963).[1] With this theme Walser continues a line of tradition in German literature, whose most prominent examples are encountered in Robert Walser's novel *Der Gehülfe* (1907; The Servant), Bertolt Brecht's didactical play *Herr Puntila und sein Knecht Matti* (1948; *Matti and Puntila, His Hired Man*, 1976), and, furthermore, in the literature of the former German Democratic Republic, Volker Braun's *Hinze-Kunze-Roman* (1985; A Hinze-Kunze-Novel).[2]

Appropriately to its tripartite structure, *Seelenarbeit* recounts the three last months of the chauffeur Xaver Zürn before his professional demotion. Xaver answers directly to Dr. Gleitze, the director of a company that manufactures security systems. Although Xaver prides himself in what he believes to be a prestigious position among the company's 497 employees (SA 226), he lives in disharmony both with himself and with the outside world. Yet while he shares his mental agony with Walser's other protagonists, Xaver constitutes an exception in that he also suffers physically, that is, from chronic constipation.

In *Seelenarbeit* Walser employs the strategy found in all his later prose texts, allowing the gradual revelation of the protagonists' social origins and histories to serve as a partial explanation for their inner conflicts. Xaver, then, is the son of a peasant family; he identifies himself as the offspring of generations of servants.

---

[1] See Anthony Waine, *Martin Walser* (Munich: Text + Kritik, 1980) 120.

[2] For a survey of the master-servant theme in German literary tradition see Hans Mayer's essay "Herrschaft und Knechtschaft. Hegels Deutung, ihre literarischen Ursprünge und Folgen," *Jahrbuch der deutschen Schillergesellschaft* 15 (1971): 251-79.

For him the history of his country is inextricably interrelated with that of his family, and so he traces the Zürn's cup of sorrow to the defeated peasant risings of the sixteenth century. His grandfather's early death in 1912 — facing bankruptcy he had committed suicide — is a further indication of his family's misfortune. As the hardest blow of fate, however, Xaver laments the death of his beloved brother Johann in World War II.[3] In the face of these childhood tragedies, his mother's rigorous pessimism seems to predict for him a lifelong misery. This is precisely the reason why Xaver has always envisioned his 'salvation' by escaping his social origins and has dreamt about his integration into the bourgeois middle class.[4] With his acceptance of a position as a mechanic in Dr. Gleitze's firm, however, his fantasies of social ascent to bourgeois 'freedom' end in proletarian subordination.[5]

Growing up fatherless and with a mother who clearly had no intention of providing a source of psychological support for the formation of her son's identity, Xaver displays the tendency to entrust himself to the care and control of male authority figures. Since Xaver has always been dependent on his superior's praise and recognition (SA 35), he has learned to value the advantages gained by obsequiousness. His relationship with his boss, however, is wrought with an ambivalence which is inexorably the consequence of a lack of positive feedback from Dr. Gleitze. Without the external approval he craves, Xaver finds no foundation on which to base the appropriateness of his actions. Thus he vacillates between two extremes: on the one hand he displays a doggish submissiveness, on the other he is only too conscious of his own powerlessness and insignificance and entertains feelings of anger and hate, even the wish to destroy people like Gleitze (SA 31).

The "schwindelhafte Ansprüche" (SA 127) [exorbitant demands] to which Xaver feels exposed manifest themselves in his work-related duties, which involve his constant availability to the Gleitzes. While Xaver admires his wife's contentment with the simple pleasures she finds in her domestic chores, he can

---

[3] Like in Günter Grass's novel *Die Blechtrommel* (1959; *The Tin Drum*, 1962), history in *Seelenarbeit* is viewed from the perspective of a lower class individual, who has experienced its pernicious effects personally. While Xaver bemoans the losses the Zürns incurred in the course of (their) history, he envies the fortune of the Gleitzes and their friends, who, coming from upper-class families never had to miss the comfort to which they are used (SA 73).

[4] These fantasies had been infiltrated into him by his brother Johann, who, Xaver is still convinced, would have steered his family's fate into a favorable direction (SH 88).

[5] See Heike Doane, "Martin Walsers *Seelenarbeit*: Versuche der Selbstverwirklichung," *Neophilologus* 67 (1983): 264.

neither emulate it nor rid himself from the feelings of alienation caused by his work role. It is this demeaning and depersonalizing relationship with Gleitze that confronts him with an insoluble conflict.

After his appointment to personal chauffeur of the director, Xaver was 'sworn in' by Dr. Gleitze (SA 18, 19) — an occurrence which preceded the events in *Seelenarbeit* by twelve years — and fancied himself at the pinnacle of his social aspirations. What he did not realize, though, is that Gleitze simply forced a clear-cut work identity upon him. Recommended as a strict non-smoker, teetotaler, and champion shot, Xaver was offered the position on account of these exquisite character attributes that assured Gleitze of Xaver's conscientiousness and reliability. Although these qualities do not correspond to reality, Xaver was emotionally overpowered by his boss's trust and confidence in him. Consequently, he submitted to and adopted his new image without resistance in the belief that his relationship with Dr. Gleitze would rest on mutual loyalty and solidarity.

An essential prerequisite in Xaver's notion of happiness is a personable and cordial intercourse with his immediate superior, essentially a relationship that disregards actual hierarchical differences. Upon realizing that he receives precisely the opposite treatment from Gleitze and is merely expected to perform according to his professional pseudo-identity, Xaver is highly disturbed. He finds it humiliating that, despite the physical closeness during their trips, it apparently never occurs to Gleitze to communicate with his chauffeur on a personal level. Yet this only intensifies Xaver's wish to share with Gleitze the event which entwined their family histories: Johann Zürn was killed during the defense of Königsberg, Gleitze's home town. By communicating this important part of his personal history to Gleitze, Xaver hopes to kindle his boss's curiosity, come to terms with past losses, overcome the distance to Gleitze, and underline the historical importance of the Zürn family. This exchange would seem to represent a confession of sorts where Gleitze's acceptance and friendship, in spite of the social disparity which exists between them, would hold the power to absolve Xaver from the Zürn legacy of failure. Because there does not seem to arise an opportunity to start this much longed-for conversation, however, all dialogue with Gleitze is confined to Xaver's mind.

The plot of *Seelenarbeit* begins where Xaver's alienation from his boss, as well as his progressive loss of self-esteem, have reached a crucial stage. Resulting from his long history of self-discipline, Xaver's illness constitutes the novel's ironic structure. He has internalized Dr. Gleitze's measures of conditioning and has suppressed his own personality by conforming to the work role imposed on him.[6] In fact, self-control for him has become second nature (SA 16). Thus, Xaver, in an even more radical fashion than Franz Horn, embodies what Marcuse has termed "the pure form of servitude" in a capitalist system: "to exist as an instrument, as a thing."[7] By the same token Dr. Gleitze demonstrates the entrepreneur's "more rational utilization of power," namely that rationality of domination that is "exercised by a particular group or individual in order to sustain and enhance itself in a privileged position."[8]

The rebellion of Xaver's bowels, then, is a direct physical reaction against his continual self-constraints. With persistent regularity these psychosomatic pains haunt him while he is driving Dr. Gleitze. Naturally, he must repress his internal turbulences and fight his own nature.[9] Again, this does not require a special effort, for Xaver was trained already as a school boy to subject certain physical needs to the dictates of his teachers. Xaver's subjugation of his natural drives to his work role causes a severe imbalance of his libidinal life and explains his almost pathological craving for pornography. Xaver has so thoroughly subjugated his powers of valuation that he can experience only the most twisted sense of vindication: it is himself whom he would like to see punished for the injustice he has suffered. This is why he hopes to compensate for having to suppress certain natural urges by indulging excessively in others, such as eating (SA 145, 274), which, of course, does anything but alleviate his bellyaches on his trips with Dr. Gleitze.

Xaver grasps the causes for his suffering only intuitively, not consciously. Instead of attempting changes he glorifies his work (both in public and to himself) and practices the "Lob der Unterdrückung" (SI 131), the ironic affirmation of his

---

[6]When, for example, Gleitze orders ice cream for Xaver in order to confirm him in his role as a teetotaler, Xaver can only dam his rage by accepting Gleitze's patronizing gesture as an indication of his boss's appreciation of his character. Later Xaver bemoans his involvement in a bar fight, which, he regrets, would not have happened had he gone to a café and eaten ice cream (SA 251).

[7]*One-Dimensional Man*, p. 33. For a discussion of Xaver's functionality see also Donna Hoffmeister, "Fantasies of Individualism: Work Reality in *Seelenarbeit*," *Martin Walser: International Perspectives*, pp. 59-70.

[8]Marcuse, *Eros and Civilization*, pp. 33-34.

[9]Cf. Peter Dettmering, "Seelenarbeit," rev. of *Seelenarbeit*, *Merkur* 33 (1979): 913. Indeed, Xaver perceives the struggle with his bowels as a "Kampf mit einem wilden Tier" (SA 30) ["battle with a wild beast"; IM 23] that he must not lose at any expense. On the other hand, Xaver associates much rather "mit Tieren als mit Menschen" (SA 11) ["with animals than with humans"; IM 5] because he feels progressively alienated from other humans.

oppressive working conditions. Like his cousin Franz Horn, Xaver perceives his identity as a negative one. It has always been his part to confirm his master's authority and dominating consciousness, while his own self-esteem is based exclusively on his functionality. Only a dim premonition reminds him that he may actually be different from what everybody considers him to be. It dawns on him that by submitting to the opinions of others about himself he became the depersonalized individual without self-respect that he is now. This self-reflection, as devastating as it may be for Xaver, for the first time disrupts his habit of insistent self-denial in that it voices his new claim to personal autonomy.[10]

Parallel to Franz Horn in *Jenseits der Liebe*, who is sent to England on business, Xaver's admittance to a hospital on Gleitze's order marks the beginning of his journey into himself, a journey of self-discovery. During his intestinal examination Xaver directly experiences his dependency on a physical level. Once again the acute degree to which he is alienated from himself is demonstrated to him when he notices the enormous distance (SA 167) between his social and genuine self. Yet, the intrusion of mechanical devices into his body enables him for the first time to detect the causality between his working conditions and his lasting discontent. After this degrading physical inspection[11] he begins to rediscover his natural sphere as a part of himself, a part, however, which has been confiscated by a foreign power. Instinctively Xaver now blames Gleitze for his malaise.[12] He dimly realizes that his hospitalization was simply another of Gleitze's tactical control measures to placate his servant's worries and assure his loyalty. For Gleitze is known to handle the "riesige Menschenmaterial" (SA 205) ["huge human reservoir"; IM 189] that stands at his disposal with the capitalist leader's ruthless calculations of profit optimization.[13]

---

[10]See Doane, "Versuche der Selbstverwirklichung," p. 265 and "Der Ausweg nach innen: Zu Martin Walsers Roman *Seelenarbeit*," *Seminar* 18 (1982): 203.

[11]Xaver feels he is treated like a defenseless animal (cf. "Tier"; "Vierbeiner"; "tierisch ohnmächtig"; SA 161, 162, 167).

[12]Xaver literally doubts the ownership of his bowels: "He, du, Darm, du, wem gehörst du eigentlich" (SA 156) ["Hey, listen, bowel! Who *do* you really belong to?"; IM 143]. Xaver compares his tortured intestines to hunted game ("edles Wild"; SA 293), while Gleitze embodies the hunter and the trainer who tames and subdues Xaver's instincts.

[13]The representative nature of Xaver's case is stressed in a twofold manner. For one, Xaver (like Franz Horn) is shown to be merely a link in a chain (extending from his predecessor via himself to his successor, from past to present to future), which seems to indicate an infinite number of possible substitutions. On the other hand, Xaver is not the only one in Gleitze's firm who is haunted by intestinal pains. One of his colleagues was 'healed' paradoxically by means of a

Since Xaver cannot penetrate the exact nature of his manipulation rationally, he remains in a defenseless and powerless position. The failure to discard his former beliefs in favor of a burgeoning intuition for the welfare of "self" leads predictably to a relapse of the self-destructiveness which characterized his former mindset. This ironic counter-logic ("logische Widersinnigkeit" SI 134) becomes apparent when his aggressions against his boss turn against himself.[14] Consequently, any potential opposition to the given conditions is automatically transformed into self-deprecation or self-reproach, and Xaver's rehearsed self-conditioning remains operative. Notwithstanding the starkly humiliating experiences at the hospital, his innate mechanisms of self-denial continue to maintain the upper hand and once again Xaver grants Gleitze total control. This retreat serves the dual purpose of subduing his murderous intentions toward Gleitze, as well as absolving himself of the necessity of acting in defense of the truth he has newly discovered. It is easier to withdraw into a shell of tortured oppressiveness in which he need only blame himself for his vile motives. After his final demotion, Xaver's self-deprecations culminate in the condemnation of himself and his family as plain "Versager" (SA 264) ["failures"; IM 247].[15]

Xaver's unconscious desire for rebellion expresses itself in his repeated battles against the temptation to buy yet another knife.[16] Despite his fears of abusing these weapons, he has succumbed several times to a purchase. Gradually his secret wish for Gleitze's destruction develops into a rational scheme. His mounting aggressions, however, are displaced and discharge in the wrong places, such as on his daughter Julia or a store owner. Hence, Xaver must brace himself with reason in order to resist the excruciating temptation to carry out what his delusions have led him to believe is a self-liberating feat, namely to become a successful individual by killing such a person as Gleitze. Eventually, however,

---

"künstlichen Anus" (SA 247) ["artificial anus"; IM 230]. Furthermore, Xaver notes, most of Gleitze's employees at some point receive medical treatment or are transferred to the same clinic (see SA 9; also Anthony Waine, "Productive Paradoxes and Parallels in Martin Walser's *Seelenarbeit*," *German Life and Letters* 34 [1980/81]: 304-05, note 5).

[14]See especially *Seelenarbeit*, pp. 144, 163, 167, 171.

[15]Like most of Walser's protagonists, Xaver experiences his own failure the more painfully as he is simultaneously confronted with the continuous success of those superior to him.

[16]See *Seelenarbeit*, pp. 32, 171, 232, 255.

the disgust with himself and his alienating work role drive him to the verge of murder only to be prevented at the last moment.[17]

Here the events take another ironic turn when Xaver's assault results in his own demotion. Resigning himself into his role as a failure, he intends to devote himself forever to his "Einübung ins Nichts" (SI 115-53) and fully agrees with his daughter, who voices similar intentions for her future working life. Shortly after Xaver begins to understand that he will never be able to accept his unconditional self-abdication, he finally rediscovers the "kaum mehr wahrnehmbares Selbstgefühl" (SA 170) ["barely perceptible sense of self"; IM 156] that had eluded him completely for quite some time. Although there exist no prospects for improvement of his situation, Xaver is able to divest himself of his Gleitze-complex. Invigorated with new reason (SA 282) Xaver buries his social aspirations as well as his envies and aggressions toward successful middle-class individuals. Although he cursorily considers suicide as a final option, his new sense of reality now prevails. He finds happiness in the natural outdoors of his farming estate and the revived affection for and intimacy with a wife who implants in him a feeling of harmony, protection, invulnerability, and security.

Naturally, Xaver's demotion to warehouse worker reinstates his proletarian status. Yet although he has unmasked his hopes of achieving personal autonomy through social ascent as self-delusion, Xaver is soon to terminate his employment at Gleitze's company. As Franz Horn reports in *Brief an Lord Liszt*, Xaver quits his job to start his own transportation business. Although he can thus pretend to be his own master, his rekindled ambition on his new quest for independence proves anything but fruitful. For Xaver himself considers it an absurd occupation to transport inanimate objects such as construction materials (SA 117). Thus his new work will subordinate him to the same alienating conditions as before, though perhaps less drastically, since the source of his perceived alienation disallows the concentration of malevolence against a specific antagonist. Once again the counter-logic inherent in Walser's conception of irony asserts itself in that Xaver's actions effect the opposite of what they intend. Nonetheless, Xaver is determined to cling tenaciously to his hopes for a "glücklichen Ausgang" (SA 191), a happy ending to his life, and seems unable to ever achieve a more objective distance toward himself and his actions.[18]

---

[17]Xaver envisions Gleitze's assassination as an act of revenge for his impeded ascent into the middle class as well as an atonement for his brother's death.

[18]Heike Doane, "Martin Walsers Ironiebegriff: Definition und Spiegelung in drei späten Prosawerken," *Monatshefte* 77 (1985): 205.

By linking his family history with that of his social class, Xaver embeds the master-servant configuration between Gleitze and himself in a historical context.[19] Hence, whenever he retells the story of his people (SA 199) with a feeling that everything is still at stake and could turn out well, he also retells the history of the underprivileged in whose favor he hopes to manipulate the course of history. In this vein, Xaver affirms the very same desire for a happy ending that Walser has expressed: "unsere Geschichte [both as story and history] anders zu erzählen, als sie in Wirklichkeit verläuft, nämlich mit dem Bedürfnis, daß es gut ausgeht"[20] [to retell a version of our (hi)story that is different from reality, in that it voices the desire for a happy ending].

Xaver's reference to the white shadow ("weißen Schatten"; SA 284) cast even by the deepest darkness coincides with Walser's testimony of his hope for democratic progress. "Der Roman, der jetzt unsere Klassengesellschaft genau darstellt, enthält die sozialistische Gesellschaft sozusagen als weißen Schatten"[21] [A novel that accurately portrays our class society contains the socialist society, as it were, as a white shadow]. Walser cannot substantiate his hopes with a concrete proposal for socio-political changes, but he wishes to kindle an awareness in the reader of the necessity for change. He hopes to sensitize the reader to social problems and initiate a concern for the question as to a happy ending of our (hi)story.

---

[19]Elvira Högemann-Ledwohn, "Mühselige Arbeit gegen den Knechtsinn," rev. of *Seelenarbeit*, *Kürbiskern* Sept. 1979: 138.

[20]Although these are Walser's own words (see Roland Lang, "Wie tief sitzt der Tick, gegen die Bank zu spielen? Interview mit Martin Walser," *Martin Walser*, ed. Klaus Siblewski [Frankfurt/M.: Suhrkamp, 1981] 56), Xaver voices the same desire (SA 192).

[21]See Konjetzky, "Gespräch mit Martin Walser," *Weimarer Beiträge* 21.7 (1975): 79.

8

The Remote-Controlled Life of Gottlieb Zürn: *Das Schwanenhaus*

LIKE HIS FICTIONAL PREDECESSORS, Dr. Gottlieb Zürn finds himself subjected to the stringent pressures of the outside world. What he furthermore shares with his cousin Xaver and his vacation lodger Helmut Halm (the Zürns are the Halms' landlords in *Ein fliehendes Pferd*) is an acute lack of self-confidence. Although Zürn makes his living as a self-employed and established real estate broker, seemingly leading a financially secure middle-class existence, he suffers from the wounds which a lifelong battle of competition has left behind.

Once again it is the protagonist's low social descent that accounts for his present middle-class malaise. Zürn's upward mobility never appeared likely at all. His father's early bankruptcy, leading subsequently to his illness and early death, left Zürn's family in dire straits. This provided the motivation for Zürn to abandon the vestiges of his proletarian existence and put an end to his family's material plight. In light of Walser's theory of the battered self-esteem of lower-class families (WS 36), Zürn's compensatory endeavors are particularly understandable. Zürn planned his social ascent with meticulous foresight. By receiving a doctoral degree of jurisprudence, he secured himself the social prestige that facilitates a successful professional career. As he admits, his sole motive has always been a voracious greed for money (SH 41). Spurred by his family's misfortune and an unparalleled petty-bourgeois inferiority complex, Zürn considers money the only means by which he can achieve both financial and psychological autonomy.

During the initial years in his profession Zürn satisfies his monetary needs as an employee of a real estate agency. Quickly married with children, his heightened social self-consciousness and increasing material expectations induce him to become self-employed. This crucial step toward professional independence, however, exposes Zürn to an even more acute pressure of financial responsibility due to the fluctuating nature of his income. Moreover, it catapults him onto the stage of free competition where the hunt for commissions becomes the sole incentive for all participants. In this vein Zürn commits himself to an existence of 'having,' the creed of which is profit maximization, acquisition, and ownership.¹ The constant pressure to maintain his competitiveness soon begins to affect all aspects of Zürn's life and blurs the confines between private and public sector.² Thus, the narrative begins at a point in Zürn's life where the ambitious aspirations that were so typical of the protagonists of Walser's earlier novels have turned into continual efforts of psychological self-assertion.

After severing his ties with the proletariat without having taken root in the middle class, Zürn finds himself in a major identity crisis. On the one hand he feels inferior to most of his bourgeois competitors and acquaintances, on the other he is nagged by feelings of guilt toward his class of origin, the class of the socially underprivileged, from which he has distanced himself financially, to which he, however, simply cannot ignore his distinct mental affinity and firm emotional bonds.³ Hence he is a representative *par excellence* of Walser's type of the petty-bourgeois 'hero,' who, despite his achievement of social ascent, cannot dissociate himself from his social origins. Since these protagonists have never learned to take risks, they consistently seek both professional and emotional stabilities.⁴ Their composed and serene exterior is usually a façade that hides the inner turmoil of their vulnerable and unstable identities.

Much like Helmut Halm, Gottlieb Zürn's main concern is to disguise and to conceal himself (SH 37, 43, 46, 47, 89, 147, 210, 219). In so doing, however, he is perpetually plagued by the fear of losing face, while continuously finding himself confronted with new challenges to master in everyday situations. Aware of his unstable identity, Zürn finds himself caught in a web of psychological

---

[1] Erich Fromm, *To Have or To Be*, World Perspectives 50 (New York: Harper & Row, 1976) 73. Fromm contrasts the two diametrically opposed modes of existence of 'Having' and 'Being' and emphasizes compulsive consumerism as the main characteristic of a Having-oriented existence. Hence modern man, who subscribes to this life style, subordinates himself to a societal super-ego and merely lives, as it were, second-hand.

[2] This is an important thematic aspect which is also reflected in the novel's structure. In each of the five chapters the scenes of Zürn's private and professional life alternate. Yet even the 'private' or 'familial' scenes are overshadowed by Zürn's reflections in his function as a real estate broker.

[3] For this reason he still feels like a stranger when traveling first-class (SH 109).

[4] Klaus Siblewski, "Die Selbstanklage als Versteck: Zu Xaver und Gottlieb Zürn," *Martin Walser*, ed. K. Siblewski (Frankfurt/M.: Suhrkamp, 1981) 170.

dependencies. Like his cousin Xaver Zürn in *Seelenarbeit*, he is dominated by an — albeit internalized — master-servant complex. Although there exist no actual social disparities among the antagonists in *Das Schwanenhaus*, Zürn thinks in hierarchical terms and constantly puts himself in relation to his competitors.

As is characteristic of Walser's protagonists, Zürn is never in accord with himself. He hopes, however, to terminate his lasting depression by securing the professional rights of sale to the Swan Villa, a gorgeous lakeside *Jugendstil* mansion, worth between two and three million Marks. This opportunity fairly bursts with both economic and social potential. The vanquishing of his main competitors Kaltammer and Schatz in the battle for this estate promises to liberate Zürn from his inferiority complex. Thus, his victory would not only affirm his own professional competence and independence, but also bring him one step closer to his ideal of achieving a state of harmony by gaining an unshakable sense of esteem in his own eyes as well as those of others.

Although Zürn is convinced of his excellent chances to succeed, he is unable to put his well laid-out plans into productive action. The mere thought of having to compete paralyzes him, making him too self-conscious to indulge in anything but incessant self-reflections. In capitulating to fear he has relinquished the very enthusiasm and spontaneity which facilitated his social rise, cultivating instead a sense of lethargic resignation. Whereas in the past he counteracted his financial limitations with energy and initiative, Zürn now shows signs of mental exhaustion from a lifelong competitive struggle. Over the years his initial material limitations, which were due to economic and professional dependencies, have given way to the compulsion to live up to his new social status in private and public appearances so as not to be stigmatized as petty-bourgeois, a concern that controls even the most personal facets of Zürn's life.

Focusing primarily on social prestige, the maintenance of publicly demanded appearances and, primarily, an impressive professional success rate, the psychological battle between independent profit hunters clearly contradicts Zürn's nature. Because in his field success depends on the ability to sell one's personality, he perceives himself as what Fromm has termed a "marketing character," to wit, "simultaneously as the seller *and* the commodity to be sold." In fact Zürn despises himself for his "complete adaptation, so as to be desirable under all conditions of the personality market."⁵ While he would rather confess his undivided allegiance to the lower classes, he vacillates between obligation and acquiescence. It certainly would be an easier, less demanding, and less 'public' position to be a member of the proletariat, but there is no way back for Zürn. His inability to recognize his desired place in society is precisely the reason for Zürn's paralyzed state ("Lähmung"; SH 7) at the beginning of the narrated events.

Similar to *Jenseits der Liebe*, the first sentence of this novel is reminiscent of Kafka's *Verwandlung*.⁶ When Walser states that the destabilized sense of self-identity is the catalyst for the plot in *Die Verwandlung* (SI 155), the same can be claimed for *Das Schwanenhaus*. Like the metamorphosed Gregor Samsa, Zürn, too, desperately tries to conceal his paralysis from his family. This necessitates the assumption of a pseudo-ego for the outside world while suppressing those emotions which constitute his real self. The resulting conflict of inner and outer world, then, causes Zürn's sullen self-reflections. Instead of focusing on practicable possibilities of self-liberation, however, Zürn's ruminations are preoccupied with his competitors. Unrelentingly, Zürn evaluates their chances of winning the quest for the Swan Villa and busies himself with designing his own master plan. Although he claims to detect shameless strategies in their advertisements,⁷ he is awed by these men, convinced — but mainly for fear of failure — that he cannot compete with them. In this vein, he interprets the successes of his competitors as an indication of his own incompetence. Because he continually disparages his own mettle, he oftentimes experiences depressions of such magnitude that he feels stripped of the capacity ever to attempt another transaction.

Zürn's indecisiveness and indolence are nourished by a lasting phase of lack of success. Due to the unsteady and uncertain nature of his income he is constantly haunted by the fear of imminent bankruptcy and the financial ruin of his family. Nevertheless, he must admit that he fares rather well financially.

---

⁵Fromm, p. 148.

⁶As for a detailed discussion of the parallels to Kafka's text see my article "Zum letzten Mal Kafka? Martin Walsers Roman *Das Schwanenhaus* im ironischen Lichte der *Verwandlung*," *Colloquia Germanica* 22 (1989): 283-95.

⁷Zürn himself, however, in a desperate attempt to outbid his competitors, eavesdrops on the negotiations between Dr. Leistle, the owner of the mansion, and Paul Schatz.

Hence, he concludes, his worries must be the result of his luxurious life style — after all, he indulges in bouts of impulsive buying —, a life style with which he, the proletarian *arrivé*, has never been in wholehearted agreement. Although he rode the post-war boom to middle-class affluence, Zürn is perturbed about the mental superiority of the new social environment. Consequently, he compulsively pretends to exude the same self-assuredness and suaveness that he so admires in his competitors in the hope that, in this fashion, he can armor himself — in Walser's terms — with a "wetterfeste Identität" (WS 50), an impervious layer of personal and social self-confidence. However, unlike Paul Schatz, Zürn is neither firmly established nor rooted in the social class in which he is professionally active. At Dr. Leistle's party Zürn feels like a total outsider in the company of an illustrious grand-bourgeois elite.[8] Owing to his inability to reconcile his past and present social environment, he can only continue to subject himself to the expectations of others and thus unwittingly, in accordance with Walser's concept of irony, pursue his own depersonalization.

Zürn has learned to conform to the opinions of his environment to such an extent that any potential desires for opposition are suffocated in their infancy. His conduct is controlled entirely by his defense mechanisms in the hope of securing himself at least what Walser calls a negative identity, that is, an identity defined by external forces.[9] Nevertheless this passive, demure, and docile identity simply represents a strategy to sustain the darwinistic struggle for survival under the laws of capitalist society.[10]

In this struggle, however, Zürn is all too easily impressed by the self-assuredness and eloquence of his peers. Their continual, glorious successes instill in him the notion that he is merely skating on thin ice. His haunting distress in financial matters, Zürn claims, is a direct consequence of his father's economic ruin. Just as his cousin Xaver in *Seelenarbeit*, Zürn believes that there is a direct link between the material sufferings in his family tradition and the concurrent

---

[8]Zürn is deeply intimidated by the other guests whom he perceives as "gut, klug, wohlriechend, verschlossen, attraktiv, unerreichbar" (SH 68) ["good, clever, fragrant, reserved, attractive, unapproachable"; SV 65].

[9]See Walser's essays on "Selbstbewußtsein und Ironie" (SI 175-96) and "Einübung ins Nichts" (SI 115-52).

[10]See R. Hinton Thomas, and Wilfried van der Will, *Der deutsche Roman und die Wohlstandsgesellschaft* (Stuttgart: Kohlhammer, 1969) 124.

historical forces, that is, Germany's economic collapse after World War I and the global economic crisis initiated by the American stock market crash of 25 October 1929. Even though he must admit that he never suffered from unexpected material lack (SH 159), Zürn cannot remedy his oversensitive petty-bourgeois money anxiety. Money assumes central importance in his life in that it becomes a material surrogate for his lack of self-esteem. Having enough money, he claims, would be total freedom, a life without pressures, life at the top, god-like untouchability (SH 87-88), in short: self-actualization.

With a relish mixed with self-disdain Zürn remembers the day when he presented his mother with his first bonus premium (10.000 Marks). By thus proving his own financial independence as well as compensating for his father's early bankruptcy, he experienced the deepest sense of satisfaction. At least within the confines of his mother's petty-bourgeois horizon, he was able to demonstrate successfully his personal autonomy. Nonetheless, Zürn realizes that he could only secure her eternal respect through her "Unterwerfung" (SH 187) ["subjection"; SV 197], and his strategy, therefore, follows an economic law.

Zürn's relationship with his former colleagues of sorts, Eitel and Meier, demonstrates the conflict between this putative economic regimen and his intuitive social affiliation. While Zürn feels a firm emotional allegiance to them, he nevertheless conscientiously keeps his distance. At each encounter he discovers a part of himself in the two social drop-outs, who enjoy their early retirement for the most part in the local pubs. Insisting on his own professional, financial, and hence social superiority, Zürn sees no possibility to fortify his middle-class consciousness by keeping their company. Thus he allows himself only superficial contact with Meier and Eitel as they provide a never-ending source of information about his main antagonist Kaltammer.

Allegedly, Kaltammer underwent a radical change from definitive Marxist persuasions to unscrupulous economic opportunism. Owing to his versatility and cunning, Kaltammer has been able to profit from any ideology; just as he assumed a leading function in the 1968 student movement, he now presents himself as a "Kapitän" [captain] on a capitalist cruise.[11] Thus his hypocritical attitudes, his ruthlessness, and opportunism, qualities that Walser quite unquestioningly presents as characteristics of the grand-bourgeois ruling class,

---

[11]Roland Lang, "Wie tief sitzt der Tick, gegen die Bank zu spielen? Interview mit Martin Walser," *Martin Walser*, ed. Klaus Siblewski (Frankfurt/M.: Suhrkamp, 1981) 54.

point to the corrupt basis of the capitalist system. Here the fundamental contradiction which constitutes Zürn's inner stratification is laid bare. While inwardly professing (an inherent) scorn for the system, Zürn has nevertheless firmly entrenched himself in the system's principles of competition and conformism. Through an unwillingness to identify himself with Kaltammer's ilk, Zürn perpetuates his self-image as being carried faultlessly by a current not by his own making. Clearly, Walser wishes to have his protagonist exculpated and considers him simply a product of extant social conditions.[12]

Zürn's life is dominated and his behavior controlled by external realities. As he becomes aware of the manipulative influence of the outside world, Zürn's own disposition toward this reality grows more ambivalent. On the one hand, albeit mainly out of his concern for the financial security of his dependents, he is inspired by the thought of marching along and actively plying the tricks of his trade. He is, however, at the same time repelled by the shameless strategies practiced by his competitors. Nevertheless he knows that honesty will not decide the bidding for the Swan Villa. Because Zürn lacks the requisite self-confidence to believe in his eventual success, he relies instead on frequent self-reminders of his presaged victory (SH 15, 18, 108). It is his hope, bordering on superstition, that his mental conviction of success can serve to elevate his thoughts from impotent plea to prophecy.

According to Walser, the main reason for Zürn's inner paralysis is that he has unmasked himself as a slave of capitalism.[13] Owing to this awareness he can no longer justify his profession with a clear conscience. As a broker he lacks an immediate function within the production process, but rather is doomed to lead a parasitic existence at the expense of others. He therefore fancies himself as that type of broker who stands for loyalty and reliability, and whose social obligation consists of mediating affordable real estate rather than such luxurious mansions as the Swan Villa. Thus Zürn constructs an internal value system which is, by definition, antithetical to the code he must embrace in order to achieve success in his profession. Predictably, then, Zürn experiences what is the physical manifestation of his internalized contradiction: it is the very will to success which

---

[12]See Lang, pp. 54-55.

[13]See Irmela Schneider, "Ansprüche an die Romanform: Ein Gespräch mit Martin Walser," *Die Rolle des Autors: Analysen und Gespräche*, ed. I. Schneider, Literaturwissenschaft — Gesellschaftswissenschaft 56 (Stuttgart: Klett, 1981) 103.

condemns him to utter motionlessness. His escapist urge to withdraw into a state of total passivity reveals the intensity of his suffering under the capitalist system and his predilection for an existence devoid of all pressure to perform. Nonetheless Zürn is too weak to forswear the given conditions. "The intellectual and emotional refusal 'to go along' appears neurotic and impotent. This is the socio-psychological aspect of the political event that marks the contemporary period: the passing of the historical forces which, at the preceding stage of industrial society, seemed to presage the possibility of new forms of existence."[14]

Only once can Zürn withstand the external pressures and preserve his personal integrity. When he deliberately ignores his appointment for negotiations with Dr. Leistle, Zürn returns home in triumph and with a sense of "Selbstverwirklichung" (SH 129) ["self-realization"; SV 131]. Here, Walser's concept of irony comes into play again. Zürn has always compulsively suppressed genuine desires in order to experience — much like Helmut Halm — his freedom of will by the conscious practice of self-denial. Now he acts against this ironic creed. Eventually of course, Zürn submits again to the professional performance pressure and heeds a second appointment to take up negotiations for the Swan Villa.

Between his two trips to Dr. Leistle, precisely in the middle of the novel's central third chapter, Zürn arrives at an essential realization. After having purchased, on impulse, a Keshan rug (one of which he already owns), he immediately condemns his expensive purchase as an act of pure irresponsibility. Zürn is struck by the knowledge that because the seductive patterns of this rug somehow reflect his notions of harmony, he has, with full intent, accepted it as a surrogate of sorts for his unfulfilled dreams of self-actualization.[15] The rugs, then, represent insignia of bourgeois culture that exile humane values to the province of the imagination and hence preclude their potential realization. Zürn's purchase thus stabilizes the very social conditions against which these values protest. While Zürn is aware that objects such as Oriental rugs can only convey

---

[14]Marcuse, *One-Dimensional Man*, pp. 9-10.

[15]Yet, the fact that his rugs are merely acquired luxury objects contradicts Zürn's idea of personal autonomy and confirms his dependency on the capitalist system. As Zürn notes, the act of buying is always a "Konsumsünde" (SH 198) ["consumer sin"; SV 209] in that it constitutes both a material gain and an idealistic loss. At least his purchase adds to his collection of luxury objects and strengthens his mental middle-class allegiance.

the illusion of a state of harmony, he nevertheless consciously seeks the shelter of illusions to escape the "Realitätsprinzip" (SH 107) ["principle of reality"; SV 106] of a performance-oriented society.

Knowing that such role playing as he practices in public (and to some extent already among his family) will further the disintegration of his personality, he enjoys visualizing an untainted, unrestrained, childlike existence in which he will find self-realization through non-goal-oriented, purposeless behavior. These desires are partly actualized in Zürn's favorite Sunday morning pastime, the playful treatment of language by writing poems, an activity that lets him productively employ genuine talents. He prudently hides his literary products from the public eye, however, and anxiously avoids exposing himself to the pressure of satisfying public standards.[16]

Another aspect of life that allows Zürn temporarily to escape the oppressive reality principle manifests itself in his aesthetic perception. Thus, the Swan Villa, with its interior decor, embodies Zürn's desires for harmony. Together with its caretaker of mythological dimensions, the wino Dionys, the mansion's erotic frescoes that represent physical fulfillment through Dionysian ecstasy exert an enticing influence on Zürn. Under their sensual-aesthetic spell he becomes oblivious to his own troubled, or rather, non-existent sex life.[17]

Nature itself constitutes another of Zürn's escape routes from the constraints imposed on him by the outside world. A scenic sight — real or imagined — suffices to put him in a state of self-oblivion and euphoric nostalgia. Although he usually unmasks his visions as self-delusion, Zürn continually indulges in his fantasies of a utopian society that has freed itself from all oppression.[18] Reality, however, refutes Zürn's dreams as being "useless, untrue — a mere play, daydreaming" because they "speak the language of the pleasure principle, of freedom from repression, of uninhibited desire and gratification."[19]

---

[16]See Siblewski, "Die Selbstanklage als Versteck," p. 175.

[17]Zürn's frustration about his own clumsiness and his wife's apparent indifference as to sexual intercourse are the reason for his obsession with pornography.

[18]Zürn describes his utopia as "Erholung der Natur, sanfter Überfluß, Entspannung als Naturprodukt ..." (SH 145) ["Nature recovering, a mild surplus, relaxation as a product of nature ..."; SV 149].

[19]Marcuse, *Eros and Civilization*, p. 129.

On an even more passionate plane, Zürn entertains his utopian desire of a regression to a pre-individual, pre-reflective, primordial state that would, in a Frommian sense, reinstate the lost existence of pure 'being.' The notion of escaping the incompleteness of his existence into a gender-combining, androgynous entity — a notion that also Helmut Halm entertains in *Brandung* — is the expression of a lack essentially sexual in definition. In physical reality, Zürn's fantasies of an identity-escape manifest themselves as the ardent urge to crawl to freedom.[20] Again, his longing is devoid of any social function and meant to lead to the actualization of his innermost impulses.[21]

The sudden awareness of the utopian nature of his self-liberating projections prepare Zürn for his crucial insights at the novel's close. Zürn must at last accept the fact that his compulsive social aspirations — both for money and public prestige — have prevented him from leading a more content existence. Only when his competitive consciousness strikes him as artificial (SH 232) can Zürn elude the 'mass psychosis of having' in which he has participated so long.[22] Finally willing to ignore the superiority of his competitors he can also relinquish his childish self-centeredness and gain a new perspective on his profession. By reducing his own standards of professional success, Zürn breaks the bubble of his utopian notions of harmony and rids himself of the imagined external pressure.

The destruction of the Swan Villa (which will make way for a new capitalist age of highrise apartments) reactivates Zürn's critical reason and helps him recognize that the confidence in his own productive skills can already grant him a certain degree of personal autonomy. Thus, Walser spares his protagonist the last stage of petty-bourgeois irony, namely the adoption of a negative identity. Zürn's self-awareness and partial self-liberation terminate his long history of self-denial. Notwithstanding the irreversibility of the given conditions of competition, he has undergone a decisive change of personality. His inner conflicts dissolve with his acceptance of his allegiance to his social class of origin, which initiates a new sense of self. Zürn's limitation of his future professional plans to the

---

[20] In the translation the double meaning of "ins Freie" (SH 213, 214) is rendered merely as "outside" and "out of the house" (SV 226).

[21] This is why Zürn's crawling must remain "sinnlos" (SH 221) ["meaningless"; SV 234] and not be exposed to the public's judgment.

[22] See Eckhard Hendscheid, "Geld macht dumm und immer dümmer," rev. of *Das Schwanenhaus*, *Frankfurter Rundschau* 23 Aug. 1980.

mediation of farming estates parallels his discovery of an inner resistance against external demands, which grants him a new reservoir of self-determination and prevents the outside world from taking absolute control over him. Zürn can face the future again with new hope and optimism.

With *Das Schwanenhaus* Walser succeeds in portraying the deformations of a middle-class consciousness under the capitalist rule of West German society of the eighties. The manipulative influence of the economic system (here the high-pressure competition of real estate brokerage) obstructs the individual's quest for self-determination. The novel's theme of the psychological aftereffects of social ascent from a petty-bourgeois viewpoint addresses relevant issues in contemporary German society. As in *Seelenarbeit*, the author presents a social order that hinders the socially underprivileged from developing a sound sense of identity. Just as in the preceding novel, Walser limits the possibility for change to the protagonist's modification of his own social expectations and self-awareness. As in the novel *Das Einhorn* there emerges in *Das Schwanenhaus* a utopia that constitutes the negative image and a protest against the criticized society. Nevertheless, while the utopia in *Das Einhorn* proves to be unrealizable and thus intensifies that novel's social criticism,[23] the critical thrust of *Das Schwanenhaus* is eventually lessened. For the protagonist's partial self-emancipation inadvertently mitigates his (and the reader's) pessimism concerning the democratization of a system that stagnates with middle-class complacency. Thus, Walser's desire for a happy ending, of which he speaks particularly in regard to *Das Schwanenhaus*,[24] is partially realized within the scope of the novel's fictional events.

---

[23]See Rainer Nägele, "Zwischen Erinnerung und Erwartung: Gesellschaftskritik und Utopie in Martin Walsers *Einhorn*," *Martin Walser*, ed. Klaus Siblewski (Frankfurt/M.: Suhrkamp, 1981) 129.

[24]See Lang, p. 56.

9

On the Prowl; or, The Existential Gloom of Gottlieb Zürn: *Jagd*

A SEQUEL TO *DAS SCHWANENHAUS*, *Jagd* returns to the life of Dr. Gottlieb Zürn after an interval of approximately a decade. Zürn, formerly an ambitious real estate broker, but perpetually intimidated and paralyzed by his more competent — and unscrupulous — competitors, meanwhile enjoys his early retirement from the toils of brokerage. Thanks to his wife Anna, who, in addition to her exhausting domestic chores, has burdened herself with her husband's professional duties — which she handles with common sense, natural competence, and unrelenting morale — Zürn can devote most of his time to his two favorite pastimes, "Nichtstun" and "Versemacherei," being idle and writing poetry (J 23), which already indicates the exclusion of immediate social conflicts from the scope of the narrated events.

As so often in Walser's novels, the social background, insofar as it concerns the protagonist, is at best implied. Evidently Zürn withdrew from the demands of his former profession as a direct consequence of his final depletion from a lifelong, grating competition that has left him in a weary, miserable, and pathetic frame of mind. Drained of all spirit, he carefully avoids human contacts, including his relatives, isolating himself in a shell of emotional atrophy: "Er hatte überhaupt nichts gegen die Menschen, er ertrug sie nur nicht mehr" (J 29) [he really carried no grudge at all against other people, he simply couldn't stand them anymore]. Although he extends the limits of his tolerance at least to immediate family members, his family life is overshadowed by Zürn's lethargy; he experiences warmth and harmony only in close contact with his trees, bushes, and his lake, perceiving himself as a sick animal waiting to be released by its death. Yet, although Zürn admits to be internally "gebrochen" (J 19) [broken], he adamantly clings to life. While material luxury has lost its formerly so miraculous effect on Zürn, he desires nothing in his existential gloom other than to be left alone.

As already seen in *Das Schwanenhaus*, Zürn's public conduct still consists of conscious role playing. On the exterior he hides his introversion and exudes a believable cheerfulness. Exhausted from the unremitting adherence to public expectations, Zürn understandably lacks the strength to oppose conformity. In hopes of eluding public demands forever, he has voluntarily subjected himself to the indisputable authority of his wife. Anna on her part commands her husband like a subordinate (J 78), a treatment which he accepts without reservations, for it rids him from any kind of responsibility and placates his painful guilt feelings in view of Anna's indefatigable efforts in the real estate business which have proved far more successful than his own former endeavors. While Zürn acknowledges Anna's unquestionable superiority and makes her into his heroine and mistress (J 29), his morale depends largely upon her recognition. Apparently he merely possesses the vacillating self-confidence of the servant, who thrives exclusively on his master's applause and appreciation of his usefulness. The master-servant theme of *Seelenarbeit*, which Walser varied in *Brandung* on an erotic plane, manifests itself in *Jagd* on a most intimate and private level.

Notwithstanding the fact that Zürn is released from the constraints of the reality principle of his profession and can enjoy a relatively high degree of personal autonomy, his frame of mind is marked by an abiding depression. In accordance with his mental comment, "Nur von dem, was fehlt, hat man ein Bewußtsein" (J 50) [One is only aware of what is missing], the narrative, that is, the protagonist's acts of perceptions, centers around the personal lack experienced by Gottlieb Zürn. This lack, then, is essentially sexual in nature — but unlike in *Ein fliehendes Pferd*, the societal underpinning of the illustrated conflict is absent. Recalling the character's sexual frustrations and his cumbersome and therefore futile attempts to seduce his wife in *Das Schwanenhaus*, one might draw the false conclusion that in *Jagd* he suffers specifically from the lack of sexual fulfillment. What Zürn actually misses, however, is not sexual activity *per se* — although his marital sex life is virtually non-existent — but rather the desire for it.[1] The aging

---

[1] Given the unambiguous association with sexual activity, the title "Jagd," which has many connotations and can be translated among others as 'hunt,' 'chase,' 'quest,' or 'pursuit,' is perhaps best rendered as 'prowl.' This connection becomes manifest in several passages. "Hast," or "Hetze" (J 65) are used synonymously. Thus the chase after the disappeared daughter Julia has merely the function of a subplot, which demonstrates Zürn's indifference with regard to family matters. Escaping the stifling atmosphere in her parents' home, Julia joins a group of maladjusted outsiders. Despite their contemptuously anti-establishment attitudes and rather inhospitable, even belligerent airs, these youngsters are portrayed in a positive light from the perspective of the weak and weary Zürn, who is simply impressed by their non-conformist life style and honest workmanship.

Zürn — he is approaching his sixties — laments the dismal fact that he can no longer enjoy erotic fantasies; on the contrary, he is even repulsed by them (J 63). While the novel's title motif with its unmistakably sexual connotations is introduced by the bustle of mating fish zipping ("jagen") through the water with the sole purpose of "Fortpflanzung" (J 7) [procreation], thus heralding their mating season, it is the appearance of Gisi Ortlieb that causes Zürn to experience a kind of second puberty as she instantly rekindles his dwindling libido. Recently remarried and hardly past her mid-thirties, Gisi startles Zürn with her overt sexual advances consisting of uninhibited, seductive, yet somewhat vulgar words and gestures. Her candidly erotic offer — herself and her friend, the forty-two-year-old Annette — rattles Zürn from his lethargy and turns his life into a restless prowl. While Zürn sorrowfully recapitulates the erotic uneventfulness of his past, he now fancies himself at the verge of the climax of his life.

Analogous to Anna, who rules Zürn in her capacity of a super-ego, Gisi takes control of Zürn's libidinal sphere, even controlling his actions and thoughts at a distance by virtue of her physical temptation. Suddenly Zürn is obsessed with a longing for, as he euphemistically puts it, "nur die der Fortpflanzung dienenden Aktionen" [only those movements that enable procreation] that he intends to practice "an ihr, mit ihr" (J 59) [on her, with her]. Although these fantasies reduce Gisi to a sex object — a degradation that she consciously promotes herself through her behavior — Zürn feels restricted by his marital ties and refuses to be guided exclusively by his instincts. Apparently hampered by society's dictates, in this case the postulate of monogamy, he resorts to his proven "Verzichtstraining" (J 59, 99) [practice of self-denial], the habitual survival strategy of Walser's ironic heroes through which they learn to accept what society refuses them.[2]

Although the yearned-for fulfillment appears his for the taking, Zürn's moral reservations prevent him from heeding Gisi's repeated invitations. Instead of becoming the "Jäger" [hunter], who ruthlessly hunts down his prey (J 61), Zürn deliberately represses his natural drives, a mechanism which instills in him a feeling of complete powerlessness and teenager-like impotence. Owing to the vexing gulf between "Wollen und Können" [desire and potential], Zürn finally begins to question society's moral norms:

---

[2]Zürn's customary credo is to resign himself to his "Wehrlosigkeit, Schwäche" (J 174) [defenselessness, weakness], a defeatist logic, which continuously ends in frustrations. This strategy proves to effect precisely the opposite of what was desired (as in Zürn's 'negotiations' with Liliane Schönherr, for example, where he walks away empty-handed) and thus follows the ironic counter-logic that Walser ascribes to petty-bourgeois irony. In the end Zürn's most hated competitor Kaltammer conquers the Schönherr mansion due to his aggressive business strategies.

Er braucht doch gar keine, also will er keine.... Wer redet ihm das ein, daß er keine braucht, keine will? Er will, daß er eine will. So sehr, wie er früher eine wollte. Die Sehnsucht nach dem Bedürfnis ist so heftig wie früher das Bedürfnis selbst. (J 62)

[He doesn't need a woman, therefore he doesn't desire one.... Who's trying to tell him that he doesn't need one, desire one? He wants himself to desire one. As much as he desired one in the past. The longing for the desire is as powerful as the desire was once itself.]

Contradicting the standards set by a societally proclaimed moral code, Zürn wants to justify his rekindled libidinal drives. For lack of a genuine sense of self-esteem, he hopes he can at least cherish his — purported but unacknowledged — virility (J 145), his sexual prowess in order to create a new existential value for himself.[3]

At last, after overcoming the wall of inhibitions erected during decades of self-prevention, Anna's distant, yet domineering control, and his personal scruples, Zürn finds himself only moments away from realizing the much coveted earthly trinity (J 141). He is still plagued, however, by the question whether sex devoid of any emotional involvement can serve as a means to an end — namely to satisfy physical desires — and whether humans can function merely as sexual "Gebrauchsartikel" (J 105) [functional objects]. Indeed the crucial incentive for his premature departure from Annette's apartment is his observation that even sex can be contaminated by public standards, that is, it can be directed to serve practical purposes such as temporarily alleviating loneliness or discontent, seeking compensation for a life that does not grant fulfillment.[4]

---

[3]The reviewers of *Jagd* find Zürn's compulsive forbearance either tragic ("Das erotische Halali eines Feriengastes," anonymous review, *Deutsche Wochenzeitung* [New York] 24 Oct. 1988: 15) or ridiculous (Josef Görtz, "Halali," *Frankfurter Allgemeine Zeitung* [Literary Supplement] 17 Sept. 1988)

[4]Zürn arrives at this conclusion during Annette's compulsive monologue, a passage which embraces the novel's central twenty pages (J 112-135). Although the information with which this segment abounds is highly incoherent and disrupts the narrative flow of the novel almost in the fashion of a Brechtian *Verfremdungseffekt*, shattering the illusion of the reality of fiction and discontinuing the reader's identification with the characters, it provides an account of Annette's hopeless existence. A former member of the 1968 student movement in the Federal Republic and apparently arrested as well as put under continuing surveillance, Annette lives a life ruled by the paranoid delusion of still being politically persecuted. Firmly convinced she is controlled by federal authorities — she lives in constant fear of being programmed and computer-controlled by an incomprehensible, postmodern, anonymous apparatus (J 118, 119, 121, 130, 131) — she shies away from all human contacts and persistently avoids appearances in public, her chief concern being to remain unrecognized. As stated on the novel's dust jacket, her lengthy oration

When Zürn later succumbs to Liliane Schönherr's seductive efforts as part of his business strategies, he realizes the artificiality and ritualistic character of sexual acts, a scenario that appears to him to be prescribed by society. While Zürn has declared sexual fulfillment the only way to gain access to life, to grasp the meaning of life, as it were, and thus bestowed on sex the sacred status of a transcendental signified, he suddenly notes that the genital organ is not an organ to experience one*self* after all (J 159). Since life itself is a passive and self-creative process it cannot be grasped consciously, much less assigned a certain meaning, Zürn reasons. Sex, then, should be considered — like by Helmut Halm in *Ein fliehendes Pferd* — rather a physical activity designed for fitness and relaxation, but not necessarily a means for self-actualization.

These contemplations along with Annette's suicide eventually lead Zürn to believe that he has overcome his nonsensical obsession with Gisi and allow him to rediscover the value of his own privacy, his family, and, most of all, the comforting ambiance of his impressive lakeside estate. Unable to either imitate the corrupt, though profitable "richtige Weg" (J 220) [way to go] demonstrated impressively by the reckless profit hunter and Zürn's arch-rival Kaltammer, nor to resign himself to the fatal destiny of the eternally-hunted personified by Annette, Zürn decides to settle for a new realism and accept his life for what it has always been: a "Nichts" (J 172) [void], which, however, is soon to be filled with a sense of contentment resulting from the sensation of harmonious embeddedness in his outdoors environment and a new sense of community with his family.

While Annette who, like Franz Horn in *Jenseits der Liebe*, had severed all social ties and, lacking any external support, finally resorted to suicide, Zürn can once more retreat to the shelter and care of his familial bonds. In the end he even overcomes his 'erotic craze' when Gisi appears "fremd" (J 220) [alien] to him. Like in *Das Schwanenhaus,* Zürn is eventually rescued by a feeling of indifference. While he is fully cognizant of the fleeting nature of his serenity, he is at least consoled by the "Einbildung, das Treiben ruhe" (J 222) [illusion that the prowl had ended]. Although one hopes for Zürn's sake that he will be able to preserve and consolidate his new-found inner stability, Zürn is himself aware that "Dauer und Ausmaß" (J 222) [length and scope] of his new equipoise are rather indeterminate. It may only be a question of time until his existential malaise regains control of him.

---

demonstrates the irrevocable permeation of her private sphere by the political sector, which has lead to the destruction of her personality.

10

Emotional Rebellion - Political Stagnation:
Dorle und Wolf

AFTER THE PERSONAL THEMATICS of *Brandung* it is perhaps surprising to find the subsequent novella *Dorle und Wolf* freighted with unambiguously political aspects. To be sure, by 1987 the novella's theme of the division of Germany had emerged as a prominent issue in recent German fiction, both in the East and the West,[1] and had always been a personal concern of Walser himself on which he expressed his sentiments in numerous essays and interviews.[2] Since the construction of the Berlin wall in 1961 until its dismantling in 1989, Walser lamented the growing and seemingly unbridgeable gulf between East and West Germany. At the same time he also confessed his helplessness and incompetence in proposing practicable measures to remedy this situation.[3]

While Walser considered it plainly utopian that the German-German differences could be overcome (WS 100), he nevertheless voiced his hopes that one day there would exist new, different German states:

> Eines nämlich, das seinen Sozialismus nicht von der Siegermacht draufgestülpt bekommt, sondern ihn ganz und gar selber entwickeln darf; und

---

[1] See the recent article by Thomas Steinfeld and Heidrun Suhr, "Die Wiederkehr des Nationalen: Zur Diskussion um das deutschlandpolitische Engagement in der Gegenwartsliteratur," *German Quarterly* 62 (1989): 345-56. In addition to *Dorle und Wolf*, the authors discuss Peter Schneider's narrative *Der Mauerspringer* (1982; *The Wall Jumper*, 1985) and Thorsten Becker's *Die Bürgschaft* (1985; The Collateral). Other texts of the eighties that address the German question include Günter Grass' *Kopfgeburten oder die Deutschen sterben aus* (1980; *Headbirths; or, The Germans Are Dying Out*, 1982), Joachim Seyppel's novel *Die Mauer oder das Café am Hackeschen Markt* (1981; The Wall; or, the Café at Hacke Square), and Bodo Morshäuser's narrative *Die Berliner Simulation* (1983; The Berlin Simulation).

[2] The most pertinent essays are collected in the volume *Über Deutschland reden* (1988; Speaking About Germany).

[3] For example, as early as 1962, in "Deutsches Mosaik" (EL 8) and in 1977 in his essay "Über den Leser" (WS 100).

eines, das seine Entwicklung zur Demokratie nicht ausschließlich nach dem kapitalistischen Krisenrhythmus stolpern muß. (WS 100)

[On the one hand, a state upon which socialism is not imposed by the victorious power, but which is allowed to develop it autonomously; on the other hand, a state whose path toward democracy is not consistently obstructed by the crises of capitalism.]

In "Deutsches Stilleben" (Still Life of Germany), an essay dated 1986, Walser petitioned Germany's right to national unity and self-determination (GR 55, 57). Walser simply persisted in his unwillingness to regard the German division as final, opposing the opinion of most pragmatic politicians. Until 1988 Walser also believed his sentiments to be no exception. Yet he was clearly disturbed by the sheer impossibility of addressing the German question in light of the apparent irreversibility of the division of Germany.[4] But the "Phantom-Schmerz" [soul ache] evoked in Walser by the loss of East Germany after World War II caused him to reject the idea of postponing or even attempting to ignore the issue.[5] It is precisely this ache that Walser wanted to externalize in *Dorle und Wolf*. In keeping with the subjective concept of writing based on the experience of a personal lack, Walser illuminates the novella's socio-political dimension from the interior of his protagonist. The divided personality of Wolf Zieger, an East German secret agent, mirrors the predicament of Germany's split identity.

Most of the feuilleton reviews that immediately followed the publication of *Dorle und Wolf* criticized Walser for his overly simplistic and hence unconvincing politicization of the subject-matter.[6] It should be noted, however, that Walser's mediation of a political theme through the private sector is allegorical in nature and must invariably appear contrived and overstated. Thus, the novella was intended as an impulse to redress an ostensibly concluded or outlawed topic. For it is the writer's responsibility to construct implicitly a utopian formalism in order

---

[4]See Niklas Frank and Joachim Köhler, "Ich hab' so ein Stuttgart-Leipzig-Gefühl," Interview with Martin Walser, *Stern* 12 March 1987: 224.

[5]See Frank/Köhler, pp. 222, 224.

[6]See the reviews by Beatrice von Matt, "'Als wäre es das Ganze': Martin Walser: 'Dorle und Wolf,'" *Neue Zürcher Zeitung* 27 Mar. 1987, overseas edition: 51; Werner Fuld, "Ein Spion mit Sehstörungen," *Frankfurter Allgemeine Zeitung* 14 Mar. 1987; Martin Halter, "Das Dasein als fortgesetztes Weder-Noch," *Basler Zeitung* 24. Mar. 1987: 33; Joachim Haubrich, "Menschlicher Schwächeanfall," *Allgemeine Zeitung Mainz* 2 May 1987; Martin Lüdke, "Nichts Halbes, nichts Ganzes," *Die Zeit* 20 Mar. 1987; Jürgen Manthey, "Ehebruch mit Deutschland-Kummer," *Frankfurter Rundschau* 11 Apr. 1987: 2; Heinrich Vormweg, "Ausrutscher ins Absonderliche," *Süddeutsche Zeitung* 14 Apr. 1987.

to prevent the automatic adaptation of moral politics to the interests of pragmatic politicians.[7]

Employed as a local government official, Wolf Zieger executes his duties for the GDR's Security Service in the West German capital, duties that consist of supplying his employers with technological data. He obtains this information, thinking it to be vital, in exchange for rendering sexual favors to a secretary in the Bonn department of defense. The control that she exercises over him (DW 10) serves to illustrate his employers' manipulative authority. Zieger did not select this profession by choice nor for ideological reasons, but was sentenced, as it were, to his present occupation after violating the authority of a university professor. Yet in the course of the nine years that he has lived in the Federal Republic he has formed inextricable roots and developed strong patriotic feelings for Germany as a whole. He thinks that by contributing to adjust the GDR's technology to Western standards, he can help promote a *rapprochement* of the two German states.

Despite his eagerness to assume a sense of political responsibility for his native country, Zieger perceives his existence in the West as an exile to no man's land. His life is ruled by the ubiquitous pressure to disguise himself and the continuous need for stealth and concealment. "Der, der er ist, darf er nicht sein, und der, der er sein darf, ist er nicht. Also ist er niemand" (DW 52) ["The person he is, is the one he is not allowed to be, and the person he's allowed to be, he isn't. So he is nobody"; NL 44]. Zieger's dependency, his state of being controlled by a foreign power, manifests itself through the virtual absence of freedom of choice. While this restriction applies primarily to his professional life, it overshadows and calls into question his private sphere as well. Zieger's divided self, with all its inner contradictions and constrictions, recurs as a leitmotif in his one-handed piano play as well as in his frequent recourse to his literary idol, Schiller's Joan of Arc, whose desolate vacillation between patriotic sentiments and individual love causes her eventual downfall.[8]

The crack in his identity affects Zieger to such an extreme degree that he even perceives the passers-by in Bonn as "Halbierte" (DW 54) ["half-people"; NL 47], whose other halves live in East Germany. But the Germans on either side, he complains, are unaware of their incompleteness; although they are convinced that

---

[7]See Armin Ayren, "Spion für die deutsche Einheit," rev. of *Dorle und Wolf, Badische Zeitung* 4/5 Apr. 1987.

[8]See Heiko Strech, "Zwischen Patriotismus und privater Liebe," rev. of *Dorle und Wolf, Tagesanzeiger* (Zurich) 1 Apr. 1987.

they live under the best possible conditions, no one seems content. Zieger deeply regrets the fact that there exists no genuine desire for a productive exchange of ideas between the two Germanies, let alone for national unity. Instead he observes only acquiescence in the citizens' responses to their respective systems, an attitude that precludes any critical engagement in political thought. The ideological indoctrination — the explicit education toward socialism in the GDR and the invariable infiltration of capitalism in the Federal Republic — successfully undercuts democratic currents. Consequently the individual's desire for social change is stifled and with it the general receptiveness to the German question in both hemispheres.

Zieger's refusal to identify with either German extreme finally leads him to turn himself in to the West German authorities in order to escape his illegitimate status ("Illegitimität"; DW 63, 115, 116). While he has always granted his political idealism primacy over his personal life, he now turns against the GDR and its security officials and rejects an existence that seeks a balance between the private realm and political commitment. Divesting himself of all reservations, Zieger chooses his new life to begin in Dorle's conservative home town, Strümpfelbach. His voluntary renunciation of his East German identity severs him from his origins and family tradition, thereby forcing him to adjust to his loss. Since his decision also terminates his belief in his contributions to German unity, he replaces his patriotism with a private idealism, that is, his sense of unbreakable unity with Dorle.

Wolf Zieger's trial illustrates the contrary perceptions of the German division as professed by Zieger himself and rebutted by the court. While Zieger is still plagued by what he perceives as the increasing hostility between East and West (DW 148), the judge dismisses Zieger's patriotic sentiments as irrelevant. The hearing takes on an almost theatrical appearance as Zieger's punishment seems to be invariably predestined. Since the judge will only take into account the constitutional law, nothing but a guilty verdict is warranted. After all, he elaborates, West Germany has reached its final destination in history and must be protected against any encroachment from the East (DW 167-68), thereby advancing the selfsame German-German animosity that Zieger claims to have detected among the population of both German states. In fact, the judge's demonstration of how to live in one part of Germany as if it were the whole (DW 75) serves to summarily dismiss the potential existence of the German question. Thus the legal authorities manage to affirm and promote the German partition and undermine the citizens' participation in political affairs. The prevailing public opinion, then, is manipulated to coincide with that of the ruling class (represented here by the conspiracy of Zieger's lawyer, prosecutor, and judge), whose interests distinctly exclude the public desire for social and political change.[9]

Wolf Zieger's emotions became the medium for Walser's own hopes, namely that historical changes may spring from the public's emotional consciousness (WS 101). These desires, however, remain unfulfilled and unacknowledged in *Dorle und Wolf*. The psychological disturbances and anxieties experienced by Zieger at the loss of his geographic origins are shared only by his wife. Before the German unification process took its course, Walser imputed the dismissal of such sentiments as those nurtured by Wolf Zieger to the strategies of the West German government headed by the conservative Christian Democrats. On the one hand, this "Bonner CDU-Routine" (GR 9) persistently ruled out all prospects of progress with regard to the German cause. In this vein the "'cunning of reason' work[ed], as it so often did, in the interest of the powers that be. The insistence on operational and behavioral concepts turn[ed] against the efforts to free thought and behavior *from* the given reality and *for* the suppressed alternatives."[10] On the other hand, the CDU leadership basked in the historical success of Germany's unification, a success, of course, that is ultimately attributable to the people in the former German Democratic Republic.

Beyond the German problematics, then, *Dorle und Wolf* can be read as an allegory of the 'regulated' petty bourgeoisie, a theme that predominates in Walser's prose in general, and which he has linked with the question of national identity. In the essay "Händedruck mit Gespenstern" (1979; Handshake with Specters) Walser cites an earlier entry from his own diary:

> Diese Nation widerspricht sich. Ich bin unfähig, nur weil ich in der BRD lebe, nur als Bewohner der BRD zu denken und zu empfinden. Aber noch weniger kann ich mir die DDR zu eigen machen. Ich kann keinen der beiden deutschen Staaten in mir oder überhaupt verteidigen.... Suche ich nationale Bilder, um eine persönliche Lage zu rechtfertigen? Wäre es besser, die Widersprüche, in denen ich lebe, von einer Klassenlage herzuleiten? Kleinbürger! Kommt mein gestörtes Verhältnis zur Realität von der Unversöhnlichkeit der Heilsbedürfnisse und Entgeltungssehnsüchte des Kleinbürgers mit der Erfüllung versagenden Klassenrealität? (DR 15-16)

---

[9]Elsewhere Walser criticizes "die Meinung der Herrschenden" [the opinion of those in power] who are at pains to obstruct the individual citizen's "Ausbildung eines kritischen und dadurch zur Veränderung drängenden Bewußtseins vom gesellschaftlichen Zustand" (WW 10,12) [development of a critical awareness, hence the desire for change with regard to social conditions].

[10]Marcuse, *One-Dimensional Man*, pp. 15-16.

[This nation contradicts itself. I am unable to think and feel exclusively as an inhabitant of the Federal Republic just because I live in the Federal Republic. But even less so can I make the GDR a part of me. I cannot defend either German state — neither within myself, or in general.... Am I looking for national images to justify a personal condition? Would it be better to deduce those contradictions with which I live from social conditions? The petty bourgeoisie! Is my troubled relationship with reality a consequence of the fact that the petty-bourgeois citizen's need for happiness and his longings for recompensation are irreconcilable with a class reality that denies him fulfillment?]

Although Walser's political commitment must be applauded, legitimate criticism was voiced against Walser's unconditional advocacy of German unity. Notably Thomas Steinfeld and Heidrun Suhr contested that such advocacy is spurious in the absence of a social historical context. When Walser demanded, "in zwei Abkürzungen dürfen wir nicht leben wollen" (WS 10) [we must not want to live in two abbreviations], he seemed to include the entire German population. It was perhaps not entirely unreasonable to assume that one aspect of voicing such a plea is simply the critical writer's wish to fulfill his obligation of participating in the current political discourse and document in this fashion his social political commitment.

Notwithstanding this criticism of narcissism on the author's part (which should not be overestimated), Walser's novella is an appeal to the reader to participate in Germany's political scene. Zieger charges the petty-bourgeois citizens of West Germany with a general incapability or unwillingness to develop an autonomous social class-consciousness and a collective self-esteem. Such political 'inadequacy' helps perpetuate the extant conditions, conforming to the intent of the social upper class which Walser emphatically denounced in 1975: "Die herrschende Klasse aber läßt täglich betäubend laut verkünden, daß wir das Ziel unserer Geschichte erreicht hätten"[11] [Every day the ruling class makes another deafening proclamation that we have accomplished the goal of our history]. The criticized finalization of the *status quo* no doubt invokes the wish for political development and, hence, for social historical progress. Yet one must be aware that Zieger's private solution is painfully lacking in its potential to ameliorate the exposed social dilemma, and hence appears impotent to contribute either general or particular alternatives. Regardless of the meanwhile accomplished German unity, within the scope of the narrated events the prospects of improvement are

---

[11] "Überblick über unser Vermögen," *Basis* 5 (1975): 136.

entirely confined — as in Walser's first novella — to the private sector.[12] Neither Zieger nor Walser transcend their voicing nostalgic grief about the losses they suffered by the division of Germany.

Comparing Wolf Zieger to his fictional predecessors elucidates his exceptional status within Walser's prose oeuvre. He no longer represents the average citizen trapped in the production process, and surely Walser did not intend this protagonist to reflect the slice of everyday life evoked by his other characters. Although *Dorle und Wolf* again depicts an individual's deformations, the problematics are transferred from a social dimension to a national plane.[13] Walser illuminates adverse conditioning mechanisms via the public opinion sector, and not, as in his other novels, through the social production process and its alienating effects on the individual. The German cause here clearly overshadows the theme of the defenseless individual dominated by external powers. It is therefore open to debate how many readers identified with or accepted Zieger's motivation and found — as Walser would have liked to see — an issue of general interest in the thematics of this novella.[14]

Walser himself admitted to his doubts as to a more than subjective significance of the theme of *Dorle und Wolf*, finally proclaiming that his concern with the German question must be indigenous to his generation, for the younger one did not seem troubled by it.[15] Hence he suddenly was no longer assured as to the scope of the German quandary (DR 79). Walser also admitted that his commitment to a united Germany was freighted with emotionalism and could not be completely substantiated rationally.[16] Nevertheless his criticism was once

---

[12]The ending of *Dorle und Wolf* is reminiscent of *Ein fliehendes Pferd* and *Brandung*. Like Helmut Halm, Wolf Zieger feels the need to recapitulate, digest, and thus gain an objective distance from the bygone events. For him too the intimacy of his relationship with his wife remains the last retreat.

[13]See Heimo Schwilk, "In der Brandung deutscher Seelenstürme," rev. of *Dorle und Wolf*, *Christ und Welt* 20 Mar. 1987: 18.

[14]Walser generally hopes that his books contain "etwas ..., was verallgemeinerungsfähig für den Leser ist"; *Martin Walser im Gespräch mit Günter Gaus*, television interview, ARD, NDR, 1985.

[15]"Über Deutschland reden," an address delivered on 30 October 1988 in Munich (DR 76-100).

[16]Walser's "Geschichtsgefühl" (DR 99) [historical emotionalism], which he decidedly dissociates from any display of nationalism (e.g. Hellmuth Karasek and Rolf Becker, "Triumphieren nicht gelernt," Interview with Martin Walser, *Der Spiegel* 8 Oct. 1990: 291), elicited for the most part negative reactions that are summarized in *Fachdienst Germanistik* 7.1. (1989): 1-2. A supportive response was voiced by Rolf Schneider, "Die deutsche Nation als Gefühl," *Der Spiegel* 5 Dec. 1988: 30-31.

again aimed at the pragmatic politicians of West Germany, who reserved for themselves the right to treat the German question only by its non-treatment, rationalizing their dismissal of the topic as the public's opinion.

While in light of the radical political developments that began with the mass exodus of East German refugees in July, 1989 and found its glorious 'happy end' on (re)unification day, 2 October 1990, it would be a presumptuous overstatement to assign to Walser an astounding anticipation. On the other hand, the events especially since 19 November 1989 have fully endorsed Walser's "Geschichtsgefühl" since the 'gentle revolution' that took place in the streets of Leipzig and Dresden prior to that date ultimately reflects the emotional roots of the rational decisions were made in the quest for German unity.

11

Conclusion

WALSER'S TEXTS DEMONSTRATE THE protagonists' loss of self in all facets of their lives. The characters are dominated exclusively by external forces — forces which Walser calls "Gegenwelt" — and hence their compulsive ruminations that constitute these narratives are the consequence of their being in disharmony with the outside world. The restriction of the narrative perspective to the perceptions of the characters points to their subjective isolation within a system that can no longer be depicted by an omniscient narrator as a coherent, meaningful whole. The narrated figural consciousness resembles a matrix onto which the outside world is projected. This underscores the problematical depiction of reality and emphasizes the characters' state of confinement within a threatening system that determines, controls, and deforms their identities.

Although each of Walser's texts concerns itself with the protagonist's subjective state of being, the protagonist's suffering originates in the extant social conditions, more precisely, in his embeddedness within a complex system of hierarchical structures. This applies also to those texts that present the main character outside of his professional life, in particular *Ein fliehendes Pferd* and, for the most part, *Brandung*. The latter is rife with such existential issues as old age and death, yet the societal relevance is discernible — especially in view of the thematic link to *Ein fliehendes Pferd*. Similarly, Wolf Zieger's loss of his home(land) in *Dorle und Wolf* mirrors primarily a personal conflict, one which nevertheless receives a political thrust as it is projected onto the division of Germany.

In conceding their impotence in asserting an individual identity, the protagonists are faced with the impossibility of providing for their own happiness against the influence of societal conditions. With the exception of Wolf Zieger, whose activities as an East German agent also pursue personal objectives, Walser's characters are too preoccupied with maintaining their defense strategies to undertake active attempts at self-actualization. Their efforts have been paralyzed and are relegated to the status of daydreams, granting them only the most fleeting of escapes from stifling social expectations. Even a cursory reading presents the reader with ample occasion to identify circumstances which exemplify Walser's approach. In *Jenseits der Liebe* Franz Horn must realize that a system that conditions its inhabitants to be adversaries rather than allies cannot foster altruistic attitudes, but rather egocentrism and greed. Horn later describes his relationship with his competitor Liszt as a torture machine that they are bound to use on one another (BL 136). Helmut Halm perceives human intercourse as a collision of battleships (FP 37), a viewpoint that is shared by Xaver Zürn, who is disconcerted about his frigid relationship with his wife. In *Das Schwanenhaus* Xaver's cousin Gottlieb laments the professional duties which he must carry out on his daily battlefield (SH 111). Even Helmut Halm, who in *Brandung* almost exclusively devotes all his attention to his emotions, cannot ignore the academic power struggles that reign among his Californian colleagues under the façade of carefree nonchalance. In *Dorle und Wolf*, finally, it is the acute lack of mutual understanding and the vengeful hostility between the two Germanies that make life in the West unbearable for Wolf Zieger. Contrary to the unrelenting reflectiveness of Walser's other characters, the thought fragments of Meßmer contribute to a bleak picture of an existential crisis of such magnitude that the individual is diminished to the point of virtual non-existence. It seems fair to say that the image of society in Walser's later texts is still best summarized by his epigram of 1967, according to which the rules of the free market would even force a society of angels to inflict damage upon each other (H 65).

That the characters sometimes internalize their aggressions is as inevitable as the manifestation of anger against those who are the concrete representatives of an amorphously oppressive system. Franz Horn eventually becomes the victim of his murderous intent toward Thiele, an action which constitutes for him the only escape route from a ultimately intolerable existence. Helmut Halm in *Ein fliehendes Pferd* perceives life as a state of non-existence and would rather be 'history' himself (FP 30). Eventually he emerges from his apathy and in a spontaneous, half-conscious act of self-defensive violence he literally overthrows his antagonist. Nevertheless, *Brandung* finds Halm vacillating between spells of nostalgia, bitterness, and frustrated homicidal fantasies, indulging in gruesome daydreams which serve as a surrogate for his unfulfilled physical passions. While Halm never runs the risk of putting his fantasies into action, Xaver Zürn's desperation drives him to instigate a murderous attack on Dr. Gleitze which is prevented only at the very last moment. Conversely, Gottlieb Zürn implements a mitigating self-loathing in order to control his anger against his competitors. Wolf Zieger, on his part, by necessity grows to accept his utter impotence vis-à-vis legal and political authorities. His aggressions, however, find a productive outlet in the furious act of writing which he envisions at the end. Hence, Zieger, Halm, and Horn in *Brief an Lord Liszt* represent the attitude of the author, who considers the self-reflexive act of writing or narrating the sole solution by which to come to terms with external reality.

With the exception of *Jenseits der Liebe*, the protagonists' experience of their own impotence under the dictates of the system entails identical endings in all of Walser's texts discussed here. Having skated along the brink of surrendering even the last vestiges of their severely damaged identities, the characters finally learn the value of adjusting their expectations to approximate more closely societal reality. On the basis of this standpoint, that appears to be, however, only of a limited durability, they discover new vigor and pragmatic optimism from their marital relationships. After rising above the ironic operation of self-negation, they discover a new, stabilizing intimacy with their wives, whom they recognize as sincere partners for genuine communication. Thus, conjugal community constitutes a social microcosm that allows for a limited context within which the ideals of friendship, solidarity, and community can still be actualized. At the end of the dramatic version of *Ein fliehendes Pferd* Helmut Halm concludes that being married allows one to ignore the rest of the world.[1] In the milieu of society's performance norms matrimony stands as the last bastion of personal autonomy. Within this microcosm of solidarity the individual is unhindered to pursue his or her desires and opportunities for self-actualization.

Nevertheless, Walser's novels do not posit unconditional reconciliation of the individual with social reality — rather they emphasize the protagonists' resignation and partial self-liberation through their fragmentary insights into society's oppressive mechanisms. Thus Walser's characters find their way back to an 'other,' into a relationship that indeed reconciles inner and outer reality. Like the narrative perspective, however, this glimmer of hope is entirely limited to the characters' perception of reality, while the disillusioning impact of the pernicious social conditions persists. In the end the characters gain an inner strength. While they neither agree to nor rebel against the contradictions between their personal ideals and social reality, they seem to be able to fathom these contradictions. Walser's continuance of his protagonists' conflicts in sequel novels, however, demonstrates the instability of this inner balance. The lack of a broader perspective that transcends the given conditions is perhaps explained by

---

[1] Martin Walser, and Ulrich Khuon, *Ein fliehendes Pferd. Theaterstück* (Frankfurt/M.: Suhrkamp, 1985) 77.

the limited thematic focus on the petty-bourgeois protagonist for whom Walser cannot envision social alternatives.[2]

The protagonists' partial self-emancipation corresponds to the gradual awareness of their sufferings, the only happy ending considered by Walser to be warranted by reality.[3] The ending of a novel, he insists, must be related to personal experience. Walser's unwillingness to ascribe a public function to literature sheds light on his reluctance to suggest solutions. He insists instead that authors portray an accurate and honest distillment of reality and personal experience so to account for even the most subtle mental processes. In this way, Walser succeeds in indicating the awakening consciousness of his characters at the conclusion of his novels. Only when social norms are encountered with a less conforming or more inquisitive frame of mind do these norms appear modifiable. Consequently, Walser does not envision social political changes in the system resulting from the characters' development. The changes he envisions must originate in a change of attitude, reflecting the mental basis on which the system arises.

Walser's texts address the question of personal autonomy by formulating the demand for a more humane society. Personal autonomy is defined in terms of its absence, elucidated by the negative experiences of the protagonists. The question of potential social change is passed on to the reader and appeals to his receptiveness to the extant conditions in order to develop a more critical or even oppositional stance toward societally imposed demands. Only in this fashion could a literary text realize its critical potential, as the written part of the text is incomplete without the reader's efforts to bring it to life. Akin to the ideas of Wolfgang Iser, Walser considers the act of reading

> nicht Zurkenntnisnehmen, sondern Entgegnung. Der Leser antwortet. Er antwortet mit seinen eigenen Wünschen und Fürchten. Er antwortet auf die Fiktion des Schreibers mit *seiner* Fiktion. Der Leser potenziert also die Fiktion. Erst in ihm entfaltet die Fiktion ihre Protestkraft, Kritikkraft, Wunschkraft. Auch ein Buch, das kein happy end hat, zeigt durch seine Stimmung, daß es lieber gut ausginge; daß es den Zustand beklagt, der zu

---

[2]See Ulrike Hick, *Martin Walsers Prosa: Möglichkeiten des zeitgenössischen Romans unter Berücksichtigung des Realismusanspruchs*, Stuttgarter Arbeiten zur Germanistik 126, ed. Ulrich Müller, et. al. (Stuttgart: Akademischer Verlag Hans-Dieter Heinz, 1983) 203.

[3]Cf. Walser's statements in an interview with Irmela Schneider, "Ansprüche an die Romanform: Ein Gespräch mit Martin Walser," *Die Rolle des Autors: Analysen und Gespräche*, ed. Irmela Schneider, Literaturwissenschaft — Gesellschaftswissenschaft 56 (Stuttgart: Klett, 1981) 100, 105.

diesem unhappy end führte; daß es eine Wirklichkeit wünscht, in der das Ende glücklich wäre. (WS 95-96)

[not receiving, but rather responding. The reader responds. He responds with his own desires and fears. He responds to the writer's fiction with *his own* fiction. Hence the reader augments the fiction. It is through him that fiction can actualize its potential of protest, criticism, and desire. Even a book without a happy ending indicates by its tone that it would rather have a happy ending; that it deplores the conditions that lead up to its unhappy ending; that it wishes for a reality that would warrant a happy ending.]

The conscious act of negation can occur only through the reader's willingness to evaluate and respond to a literary work, and thus his response constitutes the only true measure of its value. Then art becomes both the subject and object of attempts to negate social conditions. Art is creative imagination and therefore, as Marcuse states, it envisions the reconciliation of the individual with the whole, of desire with realization, of happiness with reason. While the harmony has been removed into utopia by the established reality principle, phantasy insists that it must and can be real, that behind the illusion lies *knowledge*.[4] Walser himself refuses to concretize a perspective that would transcend the extant logic of domination. When literature portrays the given negative condition effectively, Walser insists, this is already a positive answer.[5] The writer's reaction to negative social conditions implies that there exists the potential for improving these conditions. Despite the fact that Walser's texts do not offer a utopian perspective, they contain a visionary capacity with regard to social change. It is clearly more important to elicit a recognition of a need for change, and to nurture the subsequent manifestation of this need, than to refute specific social characteristics. This is what Walser calls the text's utopian energies[6] which he believes to transcend the depicted negative state of affairs. Thus, the motivation to author a novel and the creative process of writing assume greater importance than the text's potential impact that, as Walser is convinced, cannot be attributed to the author's intent.

---

[4]Marcuse, *Eros and Civilization*, p. 130.

[5]See Klaus Konjetzky, "Gespräch mit Martin Walser," *Weimarer Beiträge* 21.7 (1975): 72.

[6]See Ulrike Hick, Interview mit Martin Walser, *Martin Walsers Prosa: Möglichkeiten des zeitgenössischen Romans unter Berücksichtigung des Realismusanspruchs*, p. 294.

Walser entertains no specific expectations, neither from his readers nor his critics. Owing to the lack of evidence as to a writer's impact on others, all that one could hope is for the literary work to reach is the reader's consciousness.[7] Undeniably Walser encourages the reader to reflect on the social relevance of literature, although his conclusions remain rather nebulous. A heightened historical consciousness, he maintains, must originate "im mitarbeitenden Leser, in der Gesellschaft ..., und das nie in Reaktion auf *einen* Autor, sondern auf alle Ausdrucksbereiche zu einer gewissen Zeit"[8] [in an involved reader, in society ..., but never in reaction to *one particular* author, but rather all vehicles of expression at a given time].

Looking back on German literature of the last two decades one must indeed attest to Walser's exceptional stance with regard to his social commitment, a stance which should clearly separate him from the generation of authors that emerged during the early seventies. Criticisms of these authors are partly justified, when their works are discredited as a playful variation of bourgeois literature. This criticism is advanced on the premise that the suffering of the protagonists is not defined as the result of the fundamental conflict between the individual's quest for personal fulfillment and the restrictive social conditions, but rather as a consequence of a general existential melancholy. The individual is not confronted with a bourgeois-capitalist system, but with society as such, an abstract and anonymous apparatus.[9] This accusation of a striking lack of social political relevance is not applicable to Walser's texts. Whereas the works of the New Subjectivity are marked by both subjective form and content, the case of Walser calls for differentiation. Despite his subjective concept of writing and narrative perspective, his novels — with the partial exception of *Brandung* — do not prove to be narcissistic self-portrayals devoid of any relevance to Germany's social reality. Although the figural narration invites the reader to identify with the main characters, the frequent, albeit subtle, disruptions of this subjective perspective allow the reader a sufficiently objective distance from the figural medium.

Since the protagonist's consciousness manifests itself as reactions to external influences, the narration implicitly contains a societal perspective. Society, then,

---

[7] See *Wie und wovon handelt Literatur*, p. 135 and *Wer ist ein Schriftsteller*, p. 42.

[8] Totten, p. 34.

[9] Roman Ritter, "Die 'Neue Innerlichkeit' — von innen und außen betrachtet," *kontext 1: Literatur und Wirklichkeit*, ed. Uwe Timm and Gerd Fuchs (Munich: Bertelsmann, 1976) 255.

unmasks itself through the thoughts, utterances, and (re)actions of the protagonists. Evidently Walser can only conditionally be categorized as a New Subjectivist. Individual alienation forms the thematic basis of his narratives, which constitutes the central theme in the works of New Subjectivity. Walser, however, focuses on the localization of the individual's deformations and extrapolates their societal causes, a property of his narratives that is lacking in the New Subjective works. In Walser's prose, society speaks through the main character's compulsive reflections and enables, even urges the reader to penetrate and analyze this seemingly subjective perspective. By the same token, the subjective restriction of the narrative perspective marks the significant difference from fictional texts by authors such as Günter Grass or Heinrich Böll, who oftentimes employ an objective narrator in an attempt to establish a more global perspective on society.[10]

New Subjectivity is often lauded for the questions it raises, questions that are mostly existential in nature.[11] It should be emphasized that Walser too leaves the reader with questions — questions, however, which bear a distinct societal relevance. Therefore the rediscovery of the subject accompanied by a turning away from socio-political themes, a tendency that has dominated German literature since the early seventies, cannot be claimed for Walser. His subjective approach investigates the realm of the *objective*, that is, society itself, whose dominance manifests itself in every sentence. Instead of closing his eyes to social issues Walser demonstrates his historical consciousness as well as his desire and efforts to continue a critical debate of the current state of affairs.[12]

Analogous to his writing concept, the dialectical movement from affliction to action (WS 41), Walser, much in a Hegelian view, considers history nothing but the progressive negation of oppression by the oppressed. Negativity denotes the negation of human identity; negating this negativity is human freedom. The freedom which is realized as dialectical or negating action is thereby essentially

---

[10] Examples are Böll's *Gruppenbild mit Dame* (1971; *Group Portrait with Lady*, 1973), a novel that is narrated by an allegedly neutral author-narrator, who functions both as a collector and reporter of the facts that eventually complete the mosaic of background information and account for the present state of affairs. In Grass's *Kopfgeburten oder die Deutschen sterben aus* (1980) the narrator (who seems identical with the author) presents the characters like on a stage from an omniscient, neutral vantage point. The reader views the events from outside and is urged to evaluate.

[11] Linda DeMeritt, *New Subjectivity and Prose Forms of Alienation: Peter Handke and Botho Strauss* (New York: Lang, 1987) 99.

[12] See Ursula Reinhold, "Zu Martin Walsers 'Seelenarbeit,'" *Sinn und Form* 32 (1980): 905.

a creation. It involves not the replacement of one given by another given, but overcoming the given in favor of what does not (yet) exist.

In his writings Walser depicts the lack of self of his protagonists as a consequence of the adverse social conditions, a causality that should initiate an awareness of the pernicious social forces in the reader (WS 42). Analogous to Walser's concept of writing, his characters too — as Helmut Halm explicitly divulges in *Brandung* (B 148) — evidence a preference for immediate experiences over political issues. This denial of social and political commitment has the effect of accentuating the protagonists' discontent in present-day culture rather than negating the motivation for a historical consciousness. Conversely, a highly subjective concern on Walser's part does exist and should not be ignored, particularly with regard to *Brandung*, where Walser avows that his personal quest for identity and self-definition represent a component of his writings.[13]

The continuity of the theme of societal domination remains unbroken in Walser's prose works until 1982. After a three-year interval of the otherwise rather productive novelist, the subsequent texts *Brandung*, *Meßmers Gedanken*, and *Jagd* lack the concrete illustration of socio-political thematics, while an existential slant preponderates. Owing to its explicitly political theme, *Dorle und Wolf* assumes a unique status in Walser's oeuvre as it shows the author's personal commitment to a specific political cause more concretely and unambiguously than any other of his previous texts. Pointing in the opposite direction, *Jagd* harks back to and amplifies the tenor of disillusionment in *Brandung*. While superficially, *Jagd* still investigates symptoms of alienation, any socio-critical aspects are distinctly overshadowed by the main character's personal woes. In a 1988 interview Walser attributes his withdrawal from illustrating social conflicts to his own "Lebensstimmung" [existential ambience].[14] It is perhaps not entirely without substance that Walser has been attacked for his ostensible political about-face from pronouncedly leftist persuasions to a more conservative stance, due to his recent affiliation with the CDU.[15] Perhaps his alleged conservatism can be perceived in his most recent prose texts as an outspoken societal resignation mixed with a portion of moderate affirmation of the present state of affairs.

---

[13]Anton Kaes, "Porträt Martin Walser. Ein Gespräch," *German Quarterly* 57 (1984): 448.

[14]Paul F. Reitze, "Mit kleinen Magneten auf Jagd nach Figuren," Interview mit Martin Walser, *Die Welt* 4 Oct. 1988: 21.

[15]Willi Winkler, "Der Besinnungstäter," *Der Spiegel* 26 Feb. 1990: 221.

Whether this tendency, however, is indicative of the author's ultimate retreat from history in his future fictional writings remains to be seen.

Works Consulted

I. Works by Martin Walser (in chronological order)

1. Prose Works

———. *Ehen in Philippsburg*. Frankfurt/M.: Suhrkamp, 1957.

———. *Halbzeit*. Frankfurt/M.: Suhrkamp, 1960.

———. *Das Einhorn*. Frankfurt/M.: Suhrkamp, 1966.

———. *Fiction*. Frankfurt/M.: Suhrkamp, 1970.

———. *Die Gallistl'sche Krankheit*. Frankfurt/M.: Suhrkamp, 1972.

———. *Der Sturz*. Frankfurt/M.: Suhrkamp, 1973.

———. *Jenseits der Liebe*. Frankfurt/M.: Suhrkamp, 1976.

———. *Ein fliehendes Pferd*. Frankfurt/M.: Suhrkamp, 1978.

———. *Der Grund zur Freude: 99 Sprüche zur Erbauung des Bewußtseins*. Düsseldorf: Eremiten Press, 1978.

———. *Seelenarbeit*. Frankfurt/M.: Suhrkamp, 1979.

———. *Das Schwanenhaus*. Frankfurt/M.: Suhrkamp, 1980.

———. *Brief an Lord Liszt*. Frankfurt/M.: Suhrkamp, 1982.

———, and Ulrich Khuon. *Ein fliehendes Pferd. Theaterstück*. Frankfurt/M.: Suhrkamp, 1985.

———. *Meßmers Gedanken.* Frankfurt/M.: Suhrkamp, 1985.

———. *Brandung.* Frankfurt/M.: Suhrkamp, 1985.

———. *Dorle und Wolf.* Frankfurt/M.: Suhrkamp, 1987.

———. *Jagd.* Frankfurt/M.: Suhrkamp, 1988.

2. Dissertation, Essays, Essay Collections

———. *Beschreibung einer Form.* Munich: Hanser, 1961.

———. *Erfahrungen und Leseerfahrungen.* Frankfurt/M.: Suhrkamp, 1965.

———. *Heimatkunde. Aufsätze und Reden.* Frankfurt/M.: Suhrkamp, 1968.

———. "Mythen, Milch und Mut." *Christ und Welt* 18 Oct. 1968: 17.

———. "Berichte aus der Klassengesellschaft." Preface. *Bottroper Protokolle.* Comp. Erika Runge. Frankfurt/M.: Suhrkamp, 1968. 7-10.

———. "Wie schwer ist es, eigene Erfahrungen zu verstehen?" *Kürbiskern* Dec. 1972: 531-33.

———. *Wie und wovon handelt Literatur? Aufsätze und Reden.* Frankfurt/M.: Suhrkamp, 1973.

———. "Bemerkungen zur Literaturkritik." *Text + Kritik* 41/42 (1974): 54-56.

———. "Rascher Überblick über unser Vermögen." *Basis* 5 (1975): 132-37.

———. "Ein Blick durchs umgekehrte Fernrohr." *Gesellschaftspolitische Aspekte in Martin Walsers Kristlein-Trilogie.* By Heike Doane. Bonn: Bouvier, 1978. 1-2.

——. *Wer ist ein Schriftsteller? Aufsätze und Reden*. Frankfurt/M.: Suhrkamp, 1979.

——. "Händedruck mit Gespenstern." 1979. *Versuch, ein Gefühl zu verstehen, und andere Versuche*. Stuttgart: Reclam, 1982. 91-104.

——. "Die Literatur der gewöhnlichen Verletzungen." *Die Würde am Werktag: Literatur der Arbeiter und Angestellten*. Ed. Martin Walser. Frankfurt/M.: Suhrkamp, 1980. 7-11.

——. *Selbstbewußtsein und Ironie. Frankfurter Vorlesungen*. Frankfurt/M.: Suhrkamp, 1981.

——. "Nachruf auf einen Verstummten." *Martin Walser*. Ed. Klaus Siblewski. Frankfurt/M.: Suhrkamp, 1981. 54-57.

——. *Liebeserklärungen*. Frankfurt/M.: Suhrkamp, 1983.

——. "Unrelenting Style." Trans. Joseph McClinton. *Robert Walser Rediscovered: Stories, Fairy-Tale Plays, and Critical Responses*. Ed. Mark Harman. Hanover and London: UP of New England, 1985. 153-68.

——. *Geständnis auf Raten*. Frankfurt/M.: Suhrkamp, 1986.

——. *Heilige Brocken: Aufsätze, Prosa, Gedichte*. Weingarten: Drumlin-Verlag, 1986.

——. "Über den Umgang mit Literatur." *Martin Walser: International Perspectives*. Ed. Jürgen E. Schlunk and Armand E. Singer. American University Studies. Series I, Germanic Languages and Literature 64. New York: Lang, 1987. 195-214.

——. "Über Deutschland reden." *Die Zeit* 4 Nov. 1988: 65-67. Repr. in *Über Deutschland reden*. Frankfurt/M.: Suhrkamp, 1988. 7-23.

——. *Über Deutschland reden*. Frankfurt/M.: Suhrkamp, 1988.

———. "Kurz in Dresden." *Die Zeit* 27 Oct. 1989: 17.

———. "Zum Stand der deutschen Dinge." *Frankfurter Allgemeine Zeitung* (Literary Supplement) 5 Dec. 1989.

———. "Vormittag eines Schriftstellers: Über Deutschland reden — und die Folgen: Warum einer keine Lust mehr hat, am Streit der Meinungen teilzunehmen." *Die Zeit.* 21 Dec. 1990: 13-14.

3. Translations of Walser's Novels

Marriage in Philippsburg. Trans. Eva Figes. Adapted by James Laughlin. Norfolk, CT: New Directions, 1961.

Runaway Horse. Trans. Leila Vennewitz. New York: Holt, 1980.

The Swan Villa. Trans. Leila Vennewitz. New York: Holt, 1982.

The Inner Man. Trans. Leila Vennewitz. New York: Holt, 1984.

Letter to Lord Liszt. Trans. Leila Vennewitz. New York: Holt, 1985.

Breakers. Trans. Leila Vennewitz. New York: Holt, 1987.

No Man's Land. Trans. Leila Vennewitz. New York: Holt, 1988.

II. Interviews

Bloch, Peter André et al. "Interview mit Martin Walser." *Gegenwartsliteratur: Mittel und Bedingungen ihrer Produktion.* Ed. P. A. Bloch. Bern and Munich: Francke, 1975. 257-71.

Brantl, Sybille. "Martin Walser: Sein Leben spricht Bände." Interview with Martin Walser. *Cosmopolitan* Oct. 1986: 32-37.

Frank, Niklas, and Joachim Köhler. "Ich hab' so ein Stuttgart-Leipzig-Gefühl." Interview with Martin Walser. *Stern* 12 Mar. 1987: 220-24.

Hick, Ulrike. Interview with Martin Walser. *Martin Walsers Prosa: Möglichkeiten des zeitgenössischen Romans unter Berücksichtigung des Realismusanspruchs*. Stuttgarter Arbeiten zur Germanistik 126. Ed. Ulrich Müller, et al. Stuttgart: Akademischer Verlag Hans-Dieter Heinz, 1983. 291-303.

Kaes, Anton. "Porträt Martin Walser. Ein Gespräch." *German Quarterly* 57 (1984): 432-49.

Karasek, Hellmuth, and Rolf Becker. "Triumphieren nicht gelernt." Interview with Martin Walser. *Der Spiegel* 8 Oct. 1990: 291-301.

Konjetzky, Klaus. "Gespräch mit Martin Walser." *Weimarer Beiträge* 21.7 (1975): 70-84.

Lang, Roland. "Wie tief sitzt der Tick, gegen die Bank zu spielen? Interview mit Martin Walser." *Martin Walser*. Ed. Klaus Siblewski. Frankfurt/M.: Suhrkamp, 1981. 45-56.

Martin Walser im Gespräch mit Günter Gaus. Television Interview. ARD. NDR. 2 Nov. 1985.

Osterle, Heinz D. "Wo viel Schatten ist, ist auch viel Licht. Eindrücke eines verhinderten Einwanderers." Interview with Martin Walser. *Bilder von Amerika: Gespräche mit deutschen Schriftstellern*. Ed. Heinz D. Osterle. Münster: Englisch Amerikanische Studien, 1987. 219-30.

Reinhold, Ursula. "Gespräch." Interview mit Martin Walser. *Tendenzen und Autoren: Zur Literatur der siebziger Jahre in der BRD*. Berlin: Dietz, 1982. 284-95.

Reitze, Paul F. Interview with Martin Walser. *Die Welt* 29 Sept. 1986: 9 and 30 Sept. 1986: 7.

———. "Mit kleinen Magneten auf Jagd nach Figuren." Interview with Martin Walser. *Die Welt* 4 Oct. 1988: 21, 23.

Schneider, Irmela. "Ansprüche an die Romanform: Ein Gespräch mit Martin Walser." *Die Rolle des Autors: Analysen und Gespräche.* Ed. Irmela Schneider. Literaturwissenschaft — Gesellschaftswissenschaft 56. Stuttgart: Klett, 1981. 99-107.

Totten, Monika. "Ein Gespräch mit Martin Walser in Neuengland." *Basis* 10 (1980): 194-214, 264. Repr. in *Martin Walser.* Ed. Klaus Siblewski. Frankfurt/M.: Suhrkamp, 1981. 25-44.

Zimmer, Dieter. "Die Überanstrengung, die das pure Existieren ist." Interview with Martin Walser. *Die Zeit* 18 May 1973: 27.

III. Other Primary Sources

Bernhard, Thomas. *Die Ursache: Eine Andeutung.* Salzburg: Residenz, 1975.

———. *Der Keller: Eine Entziehung.* Salzburg: Residenz, 1976.

———. *Der Atem: Eine Entscheidung.* Salzburg: Residenz, 1978.

———. *Die Kälte*: Eine Isolation. Salzburg: Residenz, 1981.

———. *Ein Kind.* Salzburg: Residenz, 1982

———. *Gathering Evidence. A Memoir.* Trans. David McLintock. New York: Knopf, 1985. Contains the five above works in English translation: "A Child," "An Indication of the Cause," "The Cellar: An Escape," "Breath: A Decision," "In the Cold."

Böll, Heinrich. *Gruppenbild mit Dame*. Cologne: Kiepenheuer & Witsch, 1971.

Born, Nicolas. *Die erdabgewandte Seite der Geschichte*. Reinbek: Rowohlt, 1976.

Brecht, Bertolt. *Herr Puntila und sein Knecht Matti*. 1950. Frankfurt/M.: Suhrkamp, 1973.

Frisch, Max. *Montauk*. Frankfurt/M.: Suhrkamp, 1975.

——. *Montauk*. Trans. Geoffrey Skelton. New York and London: Harcourt Brace Jovanovich, 1976.

Grass, Günter. *Kopfgeburten oder Die Deutschen sterben aus*. Darmstadt: Luchterhand, 1980.

Härtling, Peter. *Nachgetragene Liebe*. Darmstadt: Luchterhand, 1980.

Handke, Peter. *Der Chinese des Schmerzes*. Frankfurt/M.: Suhrkamp, 1983.

——. *A Moment of True Feeling*. Trans. Ralph Manheim. New York: Farrar, Straus and Giroux, 1977.

——. *Die Stunde der wahren Empfindung*. Frankfurt/M.: Suhrkamp, 1975.

Kafka, Franz. "Die Verwandlung." *Sämtliche Erzählungen*. Ed. Paul Raabe. Frankfurt/M.: Fischer, 1969. 56-99.

Strauß, Botho. *Devotion*. Trans. Sophie Wilkins. New York: Farrar, Straus and Giroux, 1979.

——. *Die Widmung*. Munich: Hanser, 1977.

Struck, Karin. *Klassenliebe*. Frankfurt/M.: Suhrkamp, 1973.

IV. Secondary Sources

Adorno, Theodor W. "Kulturkritik und Gesellschaft." *Prismen: Kulturkritik und Gesellschaft*. Frankfurt/M.: Suhrkamp, 1955. 7-31.

Ayren, Armin. "Spion für die deutsche Einheit." Rev. of *Dorle und Wolf*. *Badische Zeitung* 4/5 Apr. 1987.

Batt, Kurt. "Fortschreibung der Krise: Martin Walser." *Martin Walser*. Ed. Klaus Siblewski. Frankfurt/M.: Suhrkamp, 1981. 132-38.

Baumgart, Reinhard. "Überlebensspiel mit zwei Opfern." Rev. of *Ein fliehendes Pferd*. *Der Spiegel* 27 Feb. 1978: 198-99.

Bausinger, Hermann. "Realist Martin Walser." *Martin Walser*. Ed. Klaus Siblewski. Frankfurt/M.: Suhrkamp, 1981. 11-22.

Becker, Rolf. "Der Sturz des Franz Horn." Rev. of *Jenseits der Liebe*. *Der Spiegel* 5 Apr. 1976: 204-06.

Beckermann, Thomas. "Die neuen Freunde: Walsers Realismus der Hoffnung." *Text + Kritik* 41/42 (1974): 46-53.

—. "Epilog auf eine Romanform. Martin Walsers Roman *Halbzeit*: Mit einer kurzen Weiterführung, die Romane *Das Einhorn* und *Der Sturz* betreffend." *Martin Walser*. Ed. Klaus Siblewski. Frankfurt/M.: Suhrkamp, 1981. 74-113.

—. "'Ich bin sehr klein geworden': Versuch über Walsers 'Entblößungsverbergungssprache.'" *Martin Walser: International Perspectives*. Ed. Jürgen E. Schlunk and Armand E. Singer. American University Studies. Reihe I, Germanic Languages and Literature 64. New York: Lang, 1987. 15-27.

—. *Martin Walser oder die Zerstörung eines Musters: Literatursoziologischer Versuch über "Halbzeit"*. Abhandlungen zur Kunst-, Musik-, und Literaturwissenschaft 114. Bonn: Bouvier, 1972.

Beicken, Peter. "'Neue Subjektivität': Zur Prosa der siebziger Jahre." *Deutsche Literatur der Bundesrepublik seit 1965*. Ed. Paul Michael Lützeler and Egon Schwarz. Königstein/Ts.: Athenäum, 1980. 164-81.

Behre, Maria. "Erzählen zwischen Kierkegaard- und Nietzsche-Lektüre in Martin Walsers Novelle *Ein fliehendes Pferd*. *Literatur in Wissenschaft und Unterricht* 23 (1990): 3-18.

Bessen, Ursula. "Martin Walser — *Jenseits der Liebe*. Anmerkungen zur Aufnahme des Romans bei der literarischen Kritik." *Martin Walser*. Ed. Klaus Siblewski. Frankfurt/M.: Suhrkamp, 1981. 169-83.

Blocher, Friedrich K. "Unter dem Diktat des Scheins: Zu Walsers 'Ein fliehendes Pferd.'" *Identitätserfahrung: Literarische Beiträge von Goethe bis zu Walser*. Pahl-Rugenstein Hochschulschriften. Gesellschafts- und Naturwissenschaften 157. Cologne: Pahl-Rugenstein, 1984. 85-96.

Böll, Heinrich. "Versuch über die Vernunft der Poesie." *Heinrich Böll Werke: Essayistische Schriften und Reden 3*. Ed. Bernd Balzer. Cologne: Kiepenheuer & Witsch, 1979. 34-50.

Bohn, Volker. "Ein genau geschlagener Zirkel: Über 'Ein fliehendes Pferd.'" *Martin Walser*. Ed. Klaus Siblewski. Frankfurt/M.: Suhrkamp, 1981. 150-68.

Breier, Harald. "Brando Malvolio, ein Mann von (fünfund)fünfzig Jahren: Form und Funktion des Zitats in Martin Walsers Roman *Brandung*. *Literatur in Wissenschaft und Unterricht* 21 (1988): 191-201.

Bronsen, David. "Autobiographien der siebziger Jahre: Berühmte Schriftsteller befragen ihre Vergangenheit." *Deutsche Literatur der Bundesrepublik seit 1965*. Ed. Paul Michael Lützeler and Egon Schwarz. Königstein/Ts.: Athenäum, 1980. 202-14.

Bullivant, Keith. *Realism Today: Aspects of the Contemporary German Novel*. Leamington Spa, Hamburg, New York: Berg, 1987.

Clark, Jonathan P. "A Subjective Confrontation with the German Past in *Ein fliehendes Pferd.*" *Martin Walser: International Perspectives*. 47-58.

Cohn, Dorrit. *Transparent Minds: Narrative Modes for Presenting Consciousness in Fiction*. Princeton: Princeton UP, 1978.

"Das erotische Halali eines Feriengastes." Rev. of *Jagd*. *Deutsche Wochenzeitung* (New York) 24 Oct. 1988: 15.

Dede, Ewald. "Der mißverstandene Realismus: Über Martin Walsers Romane 'Die Gallistl'sche Krankheit' und 'Jenseits der Liebe.'" *Literarische Hefte* 52 (1976): 72-90.

DeMeritt, Linda C. *New Subjectivity and Prose Forms of Alienation: Peter Handke and Botho Strauss*. Studies in Modern German Literature 5. New York: Lang, 1987.

Demetz, Peter. "Martin Walser: Analyzing Everyman." *After the Fires: Recent Writings in the Germanies, Austria, and Switzerland*. San Diego: Harcourt Brace Jovanovich, 1986. 349-61.

———. "Martin Walsers Groteske ohne Ende." Rev. of *Brief an Lord Liszt*. *Frankfurter Allgemeine Zeitung* 11 Sept. 1982.

Dettmering, Peter. "Seelenarbeit." *Merkur* 33 (1979): 911-14.

Dierks, Manfred. "'Nur durch Zustimmung kommst du weg': Martin Walsers Ironie-Konzept und 'Ein fliehendes Pferd.'" *Literatur für Leser* 7 (1984): 44-53.

Doane, Heike. "Der Ausweg nach innen: Zu Martin Walsers Roman *Seelenarbeit*." *Seminar* 18 (1982): 196-212.

———. "Die Anwesenheit der Macht: Horns Strategie im *Brief an Lord Liszt*." *Martin Walser: International Perspectives*. 81-102.

———. *Gesellschaftspolitische Aspekte in Martin Walsers Kristlein-Trilogie*. Bonn: Bouvier, 1978.

———. "Innen- und Außenwelt in Martin Walser's [sic] Novelle *Ein fliehendes Pferd*." *German Studies Review* 3 (1980): 69-83.

———. "Martin Walsers Ironiebegriff: Definition und Spiegelung in drei späten Prosawerken." *Monatshefte* 77 (1985): 195-212.

———. "Martin Walsers *Seelenarbeit*: Versuche der Selbstverwirklichung." *Neophilologus* 67 (1983): 262-72.

———. "Zur Intensivierung der politischen Thematik in Martin Walsers Kristlein-Trilogie." *Weimarer Beiträge* 30 (1984): 1842-51.

Durzak, Manfred. *Der deutsche Roman der Gegenwart: Entwicklungstendenzen und Voraussetzungen*. Stuttgart: Kohlhammer, 1979.

Dutschke, Manfred. "Jenseits der Wellen könnte man schwimmen — einige Bemerkungen zu Martin Walsers 'Brandung.'" *German Studies in India* 10 (1986): 1-8.

Enzensberger, Hans Magnus. "Gemeinplätze, die Neueste Literatur betreffend." *Kursbuch* 15 (1968): 187-97.

———. "Von der Unaufhaltsamkeit des Kleinbürgertums: Eine soziologische Grille." *Kursbuch* 45 (1976): 1-8.

Fachdienst Germanistik. 7.1 (1989).

Fischer, Bernd. "Walser und die Möglichkeiten moderner Erzählliteratur: Beobachtungen zum *Brief an Lord Liszt*." *Martin Walser: International Perspectives*. 103-10.

Forster, E. M. *Aspects of the Novel*. 1927. New York: Harcourt, Brace & World: 1954.

Frisch, Max. "Öffentlichkeit als Partner." 1958. *Homo faber. Kleine Prosaschriften. Gesammelte Werke in zeitlicher Folge 7.* Ed. Hans Mayer. Frankfurt/M.: Suhrkamp, 1976. 244-52.

Fromm, Erich. *To Have Or To Be?* World Perspectives 50. New York: Harper & Row, 1976.

Fuld, Werner. "Ein Spion mit Sehstörungen." Rev. of *Dorle und Wolf. Frankfurter Allgemeine Zeitung* 14 Mar. 1987.

Görtz, Franz Josef. "Halali." Rev. of *Jagd. Frankfurter Allgemeine Zeitung* (Literary Supplement) 17 Sept. 1988.

Greiner, Ulrich. "Der gute Hirte Martin Walser." Rev. of *Seelenarbeit. Frankfurter Allgemeine Zeitung* 17 Mar. 1979.

———. "Der Selbstverhinderungskünstler." Rev. of *Brandung. Die Zeit* 30 Aug. 1985.

Grössel, Hanns. "Herr Dr. Gleitze und sein Knecht Xaver." Rev. of *Seelenarbeit. Neue Rundschau* 90 (1979): 284-87.

Haase, Donald. "Martin Walser's *Ein fliehendes Pferd* and the Tradition of Repetitive Confession." *32nd Mountain Interstate Foreign Language Conference.* Ed. Gregorio C. Martín. Winston Salem, N.C., 1984. 137-44.

Halter, Martin. "Der alte Mann und das Mädchen." Rev. of *Brandung. Badische Zeitung* 11 Sept. 1985: 8.

———. "Das Dasein als fortgesetztes Weder-Noch." Rev. of *Dorle und Wolf. Basler Zeitung* 24. Mar. 1987: 33.

Hamm, Peter. "Das Prinzip Heimat." Rev. of *Seelenarbeit. Die Zeit* 16 Mar. 1979: 13.

———. "Martin Walsers Tendenz." *Martin Walser: International Perspectives.* 1-14. Ext. vers. of "Walsers Tendenz. Laudatio auf Martin Walser." *Deutsche*

Akademie für Sprache und Dichtung Darmstadt. Jahrbuch (1981/82). Heidelberg: L. Schneider, 1982. 82-90.

Haubrich, Joachim. "Menschlicher Schwächeanfall." Rev. of *Dorle und Wolf*. *Allgemeine Zeitung Mainz* 2 May 1987.

Hendscheid, Eckhard. "Geld macht dumm und immer dümmer." Rev. of *Das Schwanenhaus*. *Frankfurter Rundschau* 23 Aug. 1980.

Herzog, Sigrid. "Über den grünen Klee gelobt: Walsers 'Das fliehende Pferd' [sic] und die Kritik." *Neue Rundschau* 89 (1978): 492-95.

Hick, Ulrike. *Martin Walsers Prosa: Möglichkeiten des zeitgenössischen Romans unter Berücksichtigung des Realismusanspruchs*. Stuttgarter Arbeiten zur Germanistik 126. Ed. Ulrich Müller, et al. Stuttgart: Akademischer Verlag Hans-Dieter Heinz, 1983.

Hildesheimer, Wolfgang. "The End of Fiction." *Merkur* 30 (1976): 57-70.

Hillmann, R[oger]. "*Ein fliehendes Pferd* — A Reconsideration." *AUMLA* 65 (1986): 48-55.

Hoffmeister, Donna L. "Fantasies of Individualism: Work Reality in *Seelenarbeit*." *Martin Walser: International Perspectives*. 59-70.

Högemann-Ledwohn, Elvira. "Mühselige Arbeit gegen den Knechtsinn." Rev. of *Seelenarbeit*. *Kürbiskern* Sept. 1979: 137-40.

Horkheimer, Max, and Theodor W. Adorno. *Dialektik der Aufklärung*. 1944. Frankfurt/M.: Fischer, 1969.

Hyde, Anthony. "The Crack in Wolf's Mirror." Rev. of *No Man's Land*. *The New York Times Book Review* 22 Jan. 1989: 8-9.

Iser, Wolfgang. "Der Lesevorgang." *Rezeptionsästhetik*. 1975. Ed. Rainer Warning. Munich: Fink, 1979. 153-176.

Jaeggi, Urs. "Zwischen den Mühlsteinen: Der Kleinbürger oder die Angst vor der Geschichte." *Kursbuch* 45 (1976): 151-68.

Jansen, Angelika C. "Walser's *Ein fliehendes Pferd*: Reception and Position of the Work in Contemporary West German Society." Diss. New York University, 1982.

Karasek, Hellmuth. "Gott oder doch nur Gottlieb?" Rev. of *Das Schwanenhaus*. *Der Spiegel* 11 Aug. 1980: 131-33.

———. "Malvolio in Kalifornien." Rev. of *Brandung*. *Der Spiegel* 26 Aug. 1985: 158-59.

———. "Schattenwelt der Angestellten." Rev. of *Brief an Lord Liszt*. *Der Spiegel* 18 Oct. 1982: 244.

Kinder, Hermann. "Anselm Kristlein: Eins bis Drei — Gemeinsamkeit und Unterschied." *Text + Kritik* 41/42 (1974): 38-45.

Knorr, Herbert. "Gezähmter Löwe — fliehendes Pferd. Zu Novellen von Goethe und Martin Walser." *Literatur für Leser* 2 (1979): 139-57.

Koopmann, Helmut. "Tendenzen des deutschen Romans der siebziger Jahre." *Handbuch des deutschen Romans*. Ed. Helmut Koopmann. Düsseldorf: Bagel, 1983. 574-86; 655-56.

Kracauer, Siegfried. *Die Angestellten: Aus dem neuesten Deutschland*. 1930. Frankfurt/M.: Suhrkamp, 1980.

Kreuzer, Helmut. "Zur Literatur der siebziger Jahre in der Bundesrepublik." *Basis* 8 (1978): 7-32.

Kreuzer, Ingrid. "Martin Walser." *Deutsche Literatur der Gegenwart in Einzeldarstellungen*. Ed. Dieter Weber. Stuttgart: Kröner, 1976. 512-33.

Kurz, Paul Konrad. "Wer hat Angst vor Martin Walser?: I. Der ironische Stil" Rev. of *Brief an Lord Liszt*. *Frankfurter Hefte* 38.1 (1983): 65-66.

Laemmle, Peter. "'Lust am Untergang' oder radikale Gegen-Utopie? *Der Sturz* und seine Aufnahme in der Kritik." *Martin Walser*. Ed. Klaus Siblewski. Frankfurt/M.: Suhrkamp, 1981. 204-13.

Liewerscheidt, Dieter. "Die Anstrengung, ja zu sagen: Martin Walsers Ironie-Konzept und die Romane von 'Jenseits der Liebe' bis 'Brief an Lord Liszt.'" *Literatur für Leser* 9 (1986): 74-88.

Lüdke, Martin. "Nichts Halbes, nichts Ganzes." Rev. of *Dorle und Wolf*. *Die Zeit* 20 Mar. 1987.

———. "Wer hat Angst vor Martin Walser?: II. Kein ungeteiltes Vergnügen." *Frankfurter Hefte* 38.1 (1983): 66-69.

Manthey, Jürgen. "Ehebruch mit Deutschland-Kummer." Rev. of *Dorle und Wolf*. *Frankfurter Rundschau* 11 Apr. 1987: 2.

Marcuse, Herbert. *Eros and Civilization: A Philosophical Inquiry Into Freud*. Boston: Beacon Press, 1955.

———. *One-Dimensional Man: Studies in the Ideology of Advanced Industrial Society*. Boston: Beacon Press, 1964.

Martin, Jean-Maurice. *Untersuchungen zum Problem der Erlebten Rede. Der ursächliche Kontext der Erlebten Rede, dargestellt an Romanen Robert Walsers*. Europäische Hochschulschriften. Series I, Deutsche Sprache und Literatur 1009. Bern: Lang, 1987.

Martin Walser: International Perspectives. Ed. Jürgen E. Schlunk, and Armand E. Singer. American University Studies. Series I, Germanic Languages and Literature 64. New York: Lang, 1987.

Mayer, Hans. "Herrschaft und Knechtschaft. Hegels Deutung, ihre literarischen Ursprünge und Folgen." *Jahrbuch der deutschen Schillergesellschaft* 15 (1971): 251-79.

Mews, Siegfried. "Ein entpolitisierter Heine? Zur Rezeption Heines in Martin Walsers 'Brandung.'" *Heine-Jahrbuch* 27 (1988): 162-69.

———. "Martin Walsers *Brandung*: Ein deutscher Campusroman?" *German Quarterly* 60 (1987): 220-36.

Michel, Karl Markus. "Wir Überbauarbeiter: Ein Brief über mich und Meinesgleichen." *Kursbuch* 45 (1976): 9-27.

Möhrmann, Renate. "Der neue Parvenue: Aufsteigermentalität in Martin Walsers *Ehen in Philippsburg*." *Basis* 6 (1976): 140-60.

Moser, Tilmann. "Selbsttherapie einer schweren narziβtischen Störung." *Romane als Krankengeschichten: Über Handke, Meckel und Martin Walser*. Frankfurt/M.: Suhrkamp, 1985. 77-141.

Nägele, Rainer. "Martin Walser. Die Gesellschaft im Spiegel des Subjekts." *Zeitkritische Romane des 20. Jahrhunderts. Die Gesellschaft in der Kritik der deutschen Literatur*. Ed. Hans Wagener. Stuttgart: Reclam, 1975. 318-41.

———. "Zwischen Erinnerung und Erwartung: Gesellschaftskritik und Utopie in Martin Walsers *Einhorn*." *Martin Walser*. Ed. Klaus Siblewski. Frankfurt/M.: Suhrkamp, 1981. 114-31.

Nedregård, Johan. "Der verlorene Zwischenstecker. Über den Assoziationscharakter in Martin Walsers *Jenseits der Liebe* am Beispiel des 2. Kapitels." *Gedenkschrift für Trygve Sagen 1924-1977*. Ed. Sverre Dahl, et al. Osloer Beiträge zur Germanistik 3. Oslo: Oslo UP, 1979. 162-93.

Nef, Ernst. "Das bürgerliche Bewuβtsein: hilflos. Zu Martin Walser, 'Das Schwanenhaus.'" *Schweizer Monatshefte* 60 (1980): 1044-45.

———. "Die alltägliche Deformation des bürgerlichen Heldenlebens: Zu Martin Walsers 'Seelenarbeit.'" *Schweizer Monatshefte* 59 (1979): 565-69.

Nelson, Donald F. "The Depersonalized World of Martin Walser." *German Quarterly* 42 (1969): 204-16.

Nolden, Thomas. "Der Schriftsteller als Literaturkritiker: Ein Porträt Martin Walsers." *Martin Walser: International Perspectives*. 171-83.

Nollau, Günther. "Ein 'General' beim A-3-Verkehr." Rev. of *Dorle und Wolf*. *Der Spiegel* 23 Mar. 1987: 228-30.

Parkes, Stuart. "Martin Walser: Social Critic or 'Heimatkünstler': Some Notes on His Recent Development." *New German Studies* 10 (1982): 67-82.

Pawel, Ernst. "The Empty Success of Herr Zürn." Rev. of *The Swan Villa*. *The New York Times Book Review* 10 Oct. 1982: 11, 19.

Pezold, Klaus. "Martin Walser am Übergang zu den achtziger Jahren." *Weimarer Beiträge* 30 (1984): 1830-41.

——. *Martin Walser. Seine schriftstellerische Entwicklung*. Berlin: Rütten & Loening, 1971.

Pickar, Gertrud B. "Martin Walser: The Hero of Accomodation." *Monatshefte* 62 (1970): 357-66.

Pilipp, Frank. "Zum letzten Mal Kafka? Martin Walsers Roman *Das Schwanenhaus* im ironischen Lichte der *Verwandlung*." *Colloquia Germanica* 22 (1989): 283-95.

Poulet, Georges. "Phenomenology of Reading." *New Literary History* 1 (1969): 53-68.

Reich-Ranicki, Marcel. "Martin Walser." *Entgegnung. Zur deutschen Literatur der siebziger Jahre*. Stuttgart: Deutsche Verlags-Anstalt, 1979. 175-89.

Reinhold, Ursula. "Erfahrung und Realismus: Über Martin Walser." *Weimarer Beiträge* 21.7 (1975): 85-104.

———. *Herausforderung Literatur: Entwicklungsprobleme der demokratischen und sozialistischen Literatur in der BRD (1965-1974)*. Berlin: Dietz, 1976. (As to Walser, see esp. pp. 277-87)

———. "Zu Walsers Romanen in den siebziger Jahren." *Tendenzen und Autoren: Zur Literatur der siebziger Jahre in der BRD*. Berlin: Dietz, 1982. 295-308.

———. "Zu Martin Walsers 'Seelenarbeit.'" *Sinn und Form* 32 (1980): 901-05.

Ritter, Roman. "Die 'Neue Innerlichkeit' — von innen und außen betrachtet." *kontext 1: Literatur und Wirklichkeit*. Ed. Uwe Timm, and Gerd Fuchs. Munich: Bertelsmann, 1976. 238-57.

Schneider, Rolf. "Die deutsche Nation als Gefühl." *Der Spiegel* 5 Dec. 1988: 30-31.

Schnell, Ralf. "Die Literatur der Bundesrepublik." *Deutsche Literaturgeschichte: Von den Anfängen bis zur Gegenwart*. Ed. Wolfgang Beutin, et al. Stuttgart: Metzler, 1979. 491-500.

Scholz, Joachim J. "Der Kapitalist als Gegentyp: Stadien der Wirtschaftswunderkritik in Walsers Romanen." *Martin Walser: International Perspectives*. 71-80.

Schwarz, Wilhelm Johannes. *Der Erzähler Martin Walser*. Bern and Munich: Francke, 1971.

Schwilk, Heimo. "In der Brandung deutscher Seelenstürme." Rev. of *Dorle und Wolf*. *Christ und Welt* 20 Mar. 1987: 18.

Seeba, Hinrich C. "Persönliches Engagement: Zur Autorenpoetik der siebziger Jahre." *Monatshefte* 73 (1981): 140-54.

Seifert, Walter. "Martin Walser: *Seelenarbeit*. Bewußtseinsanalyse und Gesellschaftskritik." *Deutsche Romane von Grimmelshausen bis Walser*. Ed. Jakob Lehmann. Königstein: Scriptor, 1982. 545-61.

Siblewski, Klaus. "Die Selbstanklage als Versteck. Zu Xaver und Gottlieb Zürn." *Martin Walser.* Ed. Klaus Siblewski. Frankfurt/M.: Suhrkamp, 1981. 169-83.

———. "Eine Trennung von sich selbst. Zur *Gallistl'schen Krankheit. Martin Walser.* Ed. Klaus Siblewski. Frankfurt/M.: Suhrkamp, 1981. 139-49.

———. "Martin Walser." *Kritisches Lexikon zur deutschsprachigen Gegenwartsliteratur.* Ed. Heinz Ludwig Arnold. Munich: Text + Kritik, 1980.

Sinka, Margit M. "The Flight Motif in Martin Walser's *Ein fliehendes Pferd.*" *Monatshefte* 74 (1982): 47-58.

Sokolov, Raymond. "German Fiction Without Fear." Rev. of *Breakers. The Wall Street Journal* 17 Nov. 1987: 36.

Stanzel, Franz. *Theorie des Erzählens.* Göttingen: Vandenhoeck & Ruprecht, 1979.

Stoiber, Edmund. "Wo bleibt Walser?" *Die Zeit* 13 Feb. 1987: 15.

Strech, Heiko. "Zwischen Patriotismus und privater Liebe." Rev. of *Dorle und Wolf. Tagesanzeiger* (Zurich) 1 Apr. 1987.

Światlowski, Zbigniew. "Die Dichtungen Martin Walsers — Selbstbefragung und Literaturexperiment." *Universitas* 35 (1980): 373-80.

Thomas, Noel L. "Martin Walser Rides Again: *Ein fliehendes Pferd.*" *Modern Languages* 60 (1979): 168-71.

Thomas, R. Hinton. "Martin Walser — The Nietzsche Connection." *German Life and Letters* 35 (1981/82): 319-28.

Thomas, R. Hinton and Wilfried van der Will. *Der deutsche Roman und die Wohlstandsgesellschaft.* Stuttgart: Kohlhammer, 1969.

Tomashevsky, Boris. "Thematics." *Russian Formalist Criticism: Four Essays*. Ed. Paul A. Olson. Trans. Lee T. Lemon, and Marion J. Reis. Lincoln: U of Nebraska Press, 1965. 62-95.

v[on] M[att], B[eatrice]. "'Als wäre es das Ganze': Martin Walser: 'Dorle und Wolf.'" *Neue Zürcher Zeitung* 27 Mar. 1987, Overseas Edition: 51.

von Matt, Peter. "In Nöten bis zum Hals." Rev. of *Meßmers Gedanken*. *Frankfurter Allgemeine Zeitung* 23 Mar. 1985.

Vormweg, Heinrich. "Ausrutscher ins Absonderliche." Rev. of *Dorle und Wolf*. *Süddeutsche Zeitung* 14 Apr. 1987.

——. "Bittersüß die Schmerzen des Alterns." Rev. of *Brandung*. *Süddeutsche Zeitung* 31 Aug. 1985: 104.

——. "Franz Horn gibt auf." Rev. of *Jenseits der Liebe*. *Merkur* 30 (1976): 483-85.

Waine, Anthony. *Martin Walser*. Munich: Text + Kritik, 1980.

——. "Martin Walser." *The Modern German Novel*. Ed. Keith Bullivant. Leamington Spa, Hamburg, New York: Berg, 1987. 259-75.

——. "Productive Paradoxes and Parallels in Martin Walser's *Seelenarbeit*." *German Life and Letters* 34 (1980/81): 297-305.

Wellershoff, Dieter. *Literatur und Veränderung*. Köln: Kiepenheuer & Witsch, 1969.

Wiethölter, Waltraud. "'Otto' — oder sind Goethes *Wahlverwandtschaften* auf den Hund gekommen? Anmerkungen zu Martin Walsers Novelle *Ein fliehendes Pferd*." *Zeitschrift für deutsche Philologie* 102 (1983): 240-59.

Winkler, Michael. "Martin Walser." *Contemporary German Fiction Writers: Second Series*. Ed. Wolfgang D. Elfe, and James Hardin. Dictionary of Literary Biography 75:Detroit: Gale, 1988. 241-48.

Winkler, Willi. "Der Besinnungstäter." *Der Spiegel* 26 Feb. 1990: 221-25.

Index

Adenauer, Konrad 1
alienation 3, 4, 7, 11, 14, 27, 35, 45, 48, 52, 53, 61, 67, 80, 85, 86, 87, 89, 115, 123, 124
allegiance 11, 13, 53, 60, 67, 94, 96, 99, 100
anonymity 38, 56, 61, 63, 73, 107, 122
apathy 50, 56, 81, 118
aristocratic 49, 59
authority 8, 41, 48, 49, 53, 55, 59, 76, 84, 87, 104, 107, 111, 119
autobiography 24, 26, 29

Becker, Thorsten, *Die Bürgschaft* 109
Bernhard, Thomas 26, 29, 30, *Der Atem* 28, *Die Kälte* 28, *Der Keller* 28, 29, *Ein Kind* 28, *Die Ursache* 28
blue collar 12, 39, 48
Böll, Heinrich 29, 123, *Gruppenbild mit Dame* 123
Born, Nicolas 26, *Die erdabgewandte Seite der Geschichte* 27
bourgeoisie 8, 9, 40, 44, 84, 98
Braun, Volker, *Hinze-Kunze-Roman* 83
Brecht, Bertolt 83, 106, *Herr Puntila und sein Knecht Matti* 83

Canetti, Elias 26
capital 12
capitalism 5, 16, 47, 55, 58-60, 62, 66, 71, 79, 86, 95, 97, 98, 110, 122
capitalist 9, 13, 15, 56, 87
communism 14, 52, 59
competition 5, 10, 12, 13, 19, 47-49, 52, 58, 62, 64, 91, 92, 97, 100, 103
concept of writing 4, 5, 20, 23, 25, 110, 123, 124
conditioning forces 8, 56, 59, 78, 85
confession 55, 68, 69, 74, 77, 78, 80, 85
conform(ism) 1, 7, 8, 10-13, 23, 37, 39, 41, 45, 54, 59, 64, 71, 73, 80, 85, 97, 104
conservatism 16, 124
conservative party (CDU) 16, 113, 124
consumer(ism) 14, 39, 41, 65, 67, 92
corruption 97

deformation(s) (psychological) 2, 10, 12, 13, 31, 37, 40, 47, 79, 101, 115, 123
degradation 58, 59
demands (societal) 10, 52, 57, 61, 65, 66, 99, 101, 120

democracy 8, 12, 14, 16, 21, 22, 41, 49, 61, 110
democratization 12, 90, 101, 112
dependency 3, 5, 10-14, 19, 20, 35, 38, 40, 60, 72, 76, 87, 93, 99, 111
depersonalization 79, 85, 87, 95, 99
Descartes, René 80
destructiveness 12, 15, 28, 48
dialectics 21, 23, 45, 53, 78, 123
dictates (public) 5, 53, 54, 66, 69, 73, 105
disillusionment 36, 68, 76, 119, 124
domination 3, 8, 15, 20, 40, 46, 52, 53, 56, 65, 77, 83, 86, 93, 97, 115, 121, 124

economic forces 1, 5, 59, 60
(en)slave(ment) 40, 97
Enzensberger, Hans Magnus 1, 22
equality 49, 58, 61, 73
existential issues 20, 35, 61, 63, 79, 80, 103, 106, 107, 117, 118, 122-124
exploitation 9, 40, 41, 73

Fichte, Johann Gottlieb 43, 44, 49
fiction 15, 23, 74, 78, 121
freedom 4, 7, 9, 54, 55, 60, 61, 64, 66, 72, 73, 96, 98, 100, 111, 123
Frisch, Max 26, 30, *Montauk* 30
function of literature 21-23, 25, 120, 122

German Democratic Republic 83, 109-118
grand bourgeoisie 10, 12, 67, 95, 97
Grass, Günter 1, 29, 123
Die Blechtrommel 84, *Kopfgeburten* 109, 123

Härtling, Peter 26, 30
Nachgetragene Liebe 30
Handke, Peter 26
Chinese des Schmerzes 27
Stunde der wahren Empfindung 27
happy ending 89, 90, 101, 120, 121
harmony 37, 45, 51, 56, 89, 93, 98-100, 103, 107, 121
Hegel, Georg Friedrich Wilhelm 43, 83
hierarchy (social) 5, 40, 49, 58, 72, 73, 85, 97, 117
historical consciousness 41, 122-124
history 3, 12, 84, 98, 112, 114, 123, 125
Hochhuth, Rolf 1
humiliation 88

Index

ideology 8, 13, 15, 28, 60, 67, 96, 111
imagination 98, 99
implied narrator 34, 47, 55
independence 12, 14, 64, 89, 91, 93, 96
industrialist(s) 8, 9, 10, 12
inferiority complex 8, 40, 49, 50, 58, 67, 72, 74, 91, 93
insignificance (individual) 27, 53, 56, 61, 84
instincts 14, 51, 60, 75, 76, 86, 87, 105
interior monologue 32, 34
internalization 36-38, 48, 51, 53, 60, 64, 66, 67, 74, 80, 85, 93, 97, 118
introversion 36, 64, 67, 68, 72, 75, 104
irony 4, 33, 42, 43-46, 50-54, 57, 59, 60, 61, 77, 80, 85, 86, 88, 89, 95, 98, 100, 105, 119
Iser, Wolfgang 23, 120
isolation 27, 75, 103, 117

Kafka, Franz 1, 45, 62
Die Verwandlung 45, 94
Kierkegaard, Søren 33, 63
Kracauer, Siegfried 39

lack (personal) 24, 43, 44, 62, 77, 78, 91, 96, 100, 104, 110, 124
language 14, 20
Lenz, Siegfried 1, 29
lethargy 103, 105
liberty 15, 65
libido 50, 51, 86, 105, 106
loyalty 11, 85, 87, 97

manipulation 88, 90
manipulative societal mechanisms 4, 5, 9, 14, 19, 22, 31, 35, 61, 63, 65, 69, 74, 97, 101, 115
Mann, Thomas 43, 44, 59
Tonio Kröger 44
Marxism 14, 96
materialism 7, 15, 58, 62, 66, 73, 96, 103
middle class 2, 4, 13, 91
Morshäuser, Bodo, *Die Berliner Simulation* 109
Müller, Adam 43, 44, 59

narcissism 25, 31, 59, 114, 122
narrated monologue 32, 34
narrative perspective 2, 16, 32-35, 36, 47, 55, 117, 119, 122, 123
negative identity 45, 46, 53, 54, 95, 100
negativity 15, 22, 43, 123
New Subjectivity 3, 25, 26-31, 122, 123
Nietzsche, Friedrich 74, 75

non-conformity 11, 104, 120
norms 50, 64-67, 73, 76, 105, 119, 120

omniscient narrator 32
opportunism 8, 96
opposition 12, 14, 54, 60, 62, 65, 88, 104, 120
oppression 3, 5, 7, 11, 13, 19, 37, 41, 45, 52, 53, 57, 62, 73, 87, 88, 99, 118, 119
optimism 71, 100, 119

perception 23, 25, 27, 35, 50, 61, 72, 99, 104, 117, 119
performance 4, 7, 14, 15, 48-51, 59, 65, 66, 68, 98, 99, 119
personal autonomy 4, 7, 12, 19, 52, 56, 57, 60, 61, 64, 87, 89, 96, 99, 100, 104, 119, 120
petty bourgeoisie esp. 39-41
pleasure principle 4, 51, 65, 99
poet 21
point of view 36 (see narrative perspective)
political alternative 52
political consciousness 11, 13, 23
pornography 86, 99
Poulet, George 23
power(ful) 8, 9, 12, 41, 54, 55, 58-60, 63, 79, 86, 87, 111
pressure 48, 50, 91, 96, 98, 111
pretense 49, 63, 75, 77
private sphere 2, 4, 5, 20, 22, 27, 38, 50, 61, 63-65, 69, 73, 92, 107, 110, 111, 115
production (industrial) 4, 13, 55, 56, 60, 61, 97, 115
productivity (efficiency) 7, 48, 49, 60, 61
profit maximization 7, 11, 58, 59, 61, 87, 92
proletariat 2, 10, 13, 39, 89, 91, 92, 94
prosperity 8
public (life) 4, 5, 22, 38, 64, 65, 92, 104
public expectations 35 (see demands, dictates)
public opinion 67, 115, 116

reader 1, 14, 22-25, 30, 32-34, 46, 55, 62, 69, 78, 90, 101, 106, 114, 115, 118, 120-123
realism 15, 21, 22, 40, 43
reality principle 4, 51, 99, 104, 121
repression 15, 16, 51, 53, 65, 67, 73, 86, 99, 105
resignation 11, 37, 46, 53, 56, 80, 93, 119, 124
resistance 62, 73, 80, 85, 101

Index

retirement 96, 103
role play 7, 10, 61, 64, 66, 68, 75, 76, 79, 85, 89, 99, 104
ruling class 10, 15, 39, 44, 59, 97, 112, 114

Schiller, Friedrich 111
Schlegel, Friedrich 43, 44
Schneider, Peter, *Lenz* 26, 27
Der Mauerspringer 109
self-actualization 1, 2, 11, 66, 78, 96, 107, 117, 119
self-assertion 2, 11, 28, 35, 48, 53, 54, 92
self-confidence 24, 37, 38, 43-46, 48-50, 57, 59, 65, 66, 72, 91, 95, 97, 104
self-deception 78, 89, 99
self-denial 45, 51, 57, 80, 87, 88, 98, 100, 105, 119
self-destruction 54, 80, 81, 88
self-determination 12, 29, 54, 101, 110
self-discovery 53, 60, 87
self-esteem 20, 35, 41, 44, 48, 52, 58, 59, 85, 91, 96, 114
self-isolation 35, 68
self-liberation 14, 54, 56, 88, 94, 100, 119
self-prevention 106
self-realization 5, 7, 8, 37, 48, 51, 52, 63, 68, 98, 99
servitude 86
sex(ual)(ity) 51, 55, 65-68, 72-74, 76, 99, 100, 104-107
Seyppel, Joachim, *Die Mauer oder das Café am Hackeschen Markt* 109
social advancement 8, 11, 26, 37, 39, 89, 91-93, 101
social change 15, 21, 22, 25, 40, 46, 54, 69, 90, 101, 112-114, 120, 121
social conditioning 3, 7, 11, 12, 38, 46, 51, 52, 60, 64, 66
Social Liberal Party (SPD) 16
social mobility 40
social stagnation 13, 15, 16, 37, 40, 69, 101
socially underprivileged 12, 21, 41, 90, 92, 101
Socrates 43, 44
solidarity 11, 58, 62, 85, 119
spontaneity 37, 93
standard of living 8, 37, 64
strategies for survival 24, 37, 63, 69, 95, 105
Strauß, Botho 26, *Die Widmung* 30
Struck, Karin, *Klassenliebe* 26
subordinate(s) 9, 12, 56, 58, 104
subordination 5, 12, 39, 45, 53, 64, 66, 84, 89, 92, 96
subservience 48, 53

suffering 36-38, 49, 55, 78, 86, 95, 98, 120, 122
suicide 12, 48, 51, 54-56, 61, 75, 77, 80, 84, 89, 107
superior(s) 38, 51, 53, 54, 67, 72, 84
superiority 58, 59, 95, 104
survival 8, 11, 37

therapeutic 21, 57, 62, 69, 78, 80

utopia(n) 4, 14, 46, 51, 67, 77, 99, 100, 101, 109, 121

Vesper, Bernward 26
victim 48

Walser, Robert 45, *Jakob von Gunten* 45
Der Gehülfe 83
Wellershoff, Dieter 22
World War I 96
World War II 1, 28, 84, 110
writer 20, 21
writing 21, 23, 26, 45, 57, 60, 61, 62, 78, 119, 121

OHIO UNIVERSITY LIBRARY

...ook as soon as you have
...id a fine it must